YORK NOTES

General Editors: Professor A.N. Jeffares (*University of Stirling*) & Professor Suheil Bushrui (*American University of Beirut*)

Charles Dickens

LITTLE DORRIT

Notes by I. D. McGowan

MA (OXFORD) PH D (STIRLING)
Lecturer in English Studies,
University of Stirling

YORK PRESS
Immeuble Esseily, Place Riad Solh, Beirut.

LONGMAN GROUP LIMITED
Longman House,
Burnt Mill,
Harlow,
Essex

First published 1984
ISBN 0 582 79212 6
**Printed in Hong Kong by
Wilture Printing Co Ltd.**

Contents

Part 1: Introduction *page* 5
The life of Charles Dickens 5
Dickens and Victorian England 11
The literary background 10
A note on the text 11

Part 2: Summaries 13
A general summary 13
Detailed summaries 16

Part 3: Commentary 51
The topical element 51
The serialisation of *Little Dorrit* 52
Structure and plot 54
Imagery 59
Characterisation 64

Part 4: Hints for study 68
Specimen questions 70
Specimen answers 71

Part 5: Suggestions for further reading 74

The author of these notes 76

Part 1
Introduction

Little Dorrit (1855-7) belongs to the second half of the long writing career which made Charles Dickens one of the most widely read, financially successful, and influential of the great English novelists. Since his own time, the status of novels in general, and the critical estimate of his work in particular, has risen considerably, so that Dickens is now widely regarded as one of the central figures of our literature. Something of his work is even familiar to people who have never read a novel, but have seen film or television adaptations in which the stories and the vivid characters of the originals are memorably preserved. Beyond even that, the adjective 'Dickensian' has passed into general use, though at different times it can suggest either the celebration of a good-hearted jollity, as in some of his Christmas scenes, or the denunciation of a society which callously tolerates the social evils which lead to human suffering. Both of these are, of course, represented in Dickens's works, but in different ways at different points in his career, and the reader must not make hasty assumptions about what will be found in a particular novel. One way of understanding how Dickens came to occupy a special position even in his own lifetime, and also of gathering some facts relevant to the creation of *Little Dorrit*, is to consider briefly his life.

The life of Charles Dickens

Charles Dickens was born on 7 February 1812 in the southern seaport of Portsmouth, the second of eight children of a clerk in the Navy Pay Office, himself the son of domestic servants of Lord Crewe. John Dickens was apparently a kindly man, but feckless in practical matters, especially with money. He had married the daughter of the Chief Conductor of Moneys in the Pay Office, who shortly after his daughter's marriage fled abroad on the discovery of his embezzlement of large funds. Money matters in one way or another overshadowed the life of young Charles. Of several places the family lived in, he seems to have been happiest at Chatham, another southern naval base, where he delighted to read exciting and marvellous stories, such as those in the *Arabian Nights*, and acquired a distaste for the gloomy, vengeful aspects of religion.

The family moved to London in 1822, where parental irresponsibility and incompetence soon led to a financial crisis: John Dickens, unable to pay his debts, was sent (like William Dorrit) to the Marshalsea prison, where most of the family joined him. Charles, meanwhile, at the age of twelve had been sent to work in a factory, labelling bottles of shoe-blacking for six shillings a week. It was not so much the physical exhaustion resulting from this as the loneliness, the humiliation at the family's shameful circumstances, even the sense of betrayal by his parents, that made this one of the crucial episodes in Dickens's life, so painful that he could hardly confide it to anyone. These early experiences did much to extend his knowledge of the lower levels in society and to mould his responses to them which later found expression in his novels.

John Dickens was in the Marshalsea for only about three months, but several more weeks passed before he removed Charles from the blacking factory and sent him to school, where he remained until the age of fifteen, although many of his formal accomplishments were in fact self-acquired.

After eighteen months as clerk in a legal office, during which he taught himself shorthand, Charles became a freelance reporter at Doctors' Commons, where for four years he observed the often ludicrous yet oppressive process of obscure, mainly ecclesiastical courts. His knowledge of the public world was extended in 1832 by his reporting of parliamentary debates, which quickly drew attention to his professional skills of observation and fluent writing. He had meanwhile fallen in love with Maria Beadnell, the daughter of a bank manager: after several years, partly as a result of her ambivalent attitude and partly because of her parents' social superiority to the pushy young journalist, the relationship ended in 1833, leaving once again a secret bitterness. When she reappeared in his life, a widow, in 1855, he incorporated many of her features in the character of Clennam's old love, Flora Finching, in *Little Dorrit*.

At this time, Dickens also began to acquire a wider reputation with his *Sketches by Boz*, many of which drew on his journalist's observation of London life; a collected volume was published on his twenty-fourth birthday. In 1836, the publishers Chapman and Hall commissioned him to write the text to accompany a series of sporting illustrations, to be published monthly, by the artist Robert Seymour. Seymour's suicide at an early stage gave Dickens a free hand with the work, and he produced out of it his first huge success, *Pickwick Papers* (1836-7), which allowed him to move from routine journalism to fiction as the basis of his career. Also in 1836 he married Catherine Hogarth, daughter of his newspaper editor, by whom he had ten children; but over the years he and his wife gradually drifted apart, and in 1858, shortly after the publication of *Little Dorrit*, they separated.

(The death of Catherine's sister Mary in 1837, at the age of seventeen, was a deep and lasting blow to Dickens which may also have had its effect on the sometimes idealised treatment of young women in his novels.)

Following the success of *Pickwick Papers*, Dickens produced several novels in rapid succession, sometimes in the early period overlapping because of his regular method of serialisation: *Oliver Twist* (1837-8), *Nicholas Nickleby* (1838-9), *The Old Curiosity Shop* (1840-1), *Barnaby Rudge* (1841). Having visited the United States, he incorporated his criticisms in the American episodes of *Martin Chuzzlewit* (1843-4). The early novels have a wide variety of settings (*Barnaby Rudge* is set in the late eighteenth century), many memorably grotesque villains and comic characters, and often focus on particular social or personal ills. During this time, Dickens greatly widened his circle of acquaintance as his fame and wealth grew. In his continental travels in 1844-5, he visited Genoa, Marseilles, Venice, Rome and Naples, as a result of which he published *Pictures from Italy* (1846), which shows a very limited interest in the monuments of classical antiquity. In 1846, he visited the Swiss Alps, and went to the Great St Bernard. These experiences, together with a little from his visits to France in the 1850s, contributed a good deal of background material for the Continental scenes of *Little Dorrit*, especially in Book the Second.

With *Dombey and Son* (1846-8), Dickens, though persisting with serial publication, improved the careful overall planning of his novels, which were increasingly to be concerned with investigations of the social and moral foundations of his world. *David Copperfield* (1849-50) looked back at his own childhood; *Bleak House* (1852-3), *Hard Times* (1854), and *Little Dorrit* (1855-7) continued the social themes. Dickens meanwhile founded and edited *Household Words*, a weekly magazine, succeeded by *All the Year Round* in 1859. Both of these contained non-fiction of general interest, including Dickens's investigative journalism, but also serialised fiction, including his *A Tale of Two Cities* (1859) and *Great Expectations* (1860-1). *Our Mutual Friend* (1864-5) was his last completed novel; he died during the serialisation of *Edwin Drood* in 1870.

In addition to his full-length novels, Dickens produced vast numbers of articles, speeches, stories; he loved amateur theatricals, and was a famous reader of his own works on tours in Britain and America, which drained even his remarkable energy. Although he enjoyed and profited financially from much of his work, he seems to have been at heart a restless man, despite his large family and his fine house at Gad's Hill, near his boyhood home at Chatham. His interest in social questions was not confined to his fiction: his attacks on various abuses and on the system which tolerated them were complemented by his support for philanthropic and reforming causes; he was particularly concerned with provision for housing and educating the poor. As his social analysis grew more comprehensive, he became increasingly impatient with the deficiencies of parliamentary government. (The reflection of this in *Little Dorrit* is discussed later.) Though he could be fierce in his condemnation of the guilty or complacent it was the depth of his humanitarian interest as well as his literary skill which won him a special place in the heart of a remarkably wide public. His death on 9 June 1870 was followed by many generous tributes, and burial in Poets' Corner in Westminster Abbey.

Dickens and Victorian England

Little Dorrit was published in 1855-7. Although the opening and various details show that, like several of his other novels, it is set in the period of his childhood, the 1820s, when his own father was imprisoned in the Marshalsea, certain features of it, as often in Dickens, clearly refer more specifically to the society in which it first appeared, as he pointedly suggests in his Preface. Both periods had of course much in common, and their blending here may usefully draw attention to Dickens's artistic methods (discussed in Part 3) and to the fact that a novel is not a straightforward historical document.

Our view of Victorian England (strictly, the period 1837-1901) seems to alternate between admiration for a time of invention and material progress, and condemnation of a complacent social elite indifferent to the sufferings of the mass of the people. Neither, of course, is wholly true: Dickens's long writing career reflects the fact that he lived in a time of considerable change, in which there was, at least in some quarters, anxious debate about where it was carrying the nation. The Industrial Revolution had since the eighteenth century been changing the nature of British society, as a largely agricultural country became dominated by the great industrial towns to which people flocked to work in ever larger factories, performing repetitive tasks involving powered machinery. The improvement in communications, especially with the spread of railways in the 1840s, produced a tendency to centralisation and homogeneity. The material benefits arising from inventions in many areas and from Britain's increasing world trade in a time of commercial and political imperialism were celebrated in the Great Exhibition in London in 1851, about which Dickens was notably unenthusiastic.

Dickens had his reservations partly because he was aware that the material benefits were not universally available: his knowledge of the life of the poor had alerted him especially to the problems of the great cities where the ill-fed and ill-educated masses huddled in slums which were the breeding-ground of disease and crime; in *Little Dorrit*, the cases of Tattycoram, Maggy, and Old Nandy show some of the problems with which small-scale institutional or personal charity had to cope. (In *Hard Times*, Dickens had already investigated the dehumanising effect of the industrial system in a northern factory town.) But Dickens was not merely concerned with material deprivation: like the social critic Thomas Carlyle, he was aware of the moral and spiritual damage sustained by individuals in an increasingly materialist, competitive world, in which one element in society seemed to triumph at the expense of another.

Victorian England had inherited much of the social hierarchy and systems of government formed under very different conditions. In the presentation of Lord Decimus Tite Barnacle and his relations, we can see the aristocratic class still clinging to a power it no longer justifies by a sense of responsibility. The social disdain with which the Barnacles' distant connection, Mrs Gowan, neatly ensconced at Hampton Court Palace, treats the middle-class Meagleses reinforces this theme. Indeed the novel is full of characters rising or falling in the world, or desperately clinging to the position they have established. You might consider in this context Mr Meagles's gratification at Pet's marriage to Henry Gowan; Mr Dorrit's shameful refusal to admit his own status in the Marshalsea, his attitude to Clennam, and his condescension to Old Nandy; Fanny's various dealings with Mrs Merdle over Edmund Sparkler; 'Society's' attitude to Mr Merdle before and after his exposure. Clearly the hierarchies are breaking down, if only slowly; but the rise of the self-made businessman, Mr Merdle, is no more reassuring than the decay of the Barnacles: a society dominated by snobbery or greed is likely to have little interest in a practical benefactor of his fellow men like Daniel Doyce (about whose factory we learn very little, but it is clearly not a large-scale operation). There are many sources of money in the novel, from Mr Dorrit's inheritance, through Casby's high rents and Sparkler's 'job' in the Circumlocution Office, to Merdle's frauds: you could try to work out what Dickens is saying about the economic basis of this society.

In the Clennam family firm Dickens shows us an old-fashioned small-scale mercantile house in decay; in Mrs Clennam herself, he embodies the less attractive side of Victorian religion—gloomy, repressive, and self-righteous—in contrast to the spirit of practical love found in Little Dorrit. Dickens was generally less interested in specific religious doctrines than in the transforming power of the Jesus described in the New Testament.

Much of the necessary social background can be gathered from the novel itself, though the modern reader needs help to discover which details are appropriate to the 1820s and which to the 1850s. (The Marshalsea, for instance, was closed in 1849, though imprisonment for debt was not abolished till twenty years later.) Our enjoyment and understanding may be heightened by reading some social history of the period or by looking at some contemporary illustrations of everyday life, to see how people dressed, where they lived. It is very useful to have a map of London handy (always remembering that despite its then astonishing size it was even in the 1850s far smaller than the present metropolitan area). Use of a map not only makes it easier to follow the movements of the characters, but reinforces the sense we get from the novel of the vast city made up of a number of communities physically and mentally separated from each other. The 'community' of the Marshalsea is south of the River Thames; Mrs Clennam's house, representative of a traditional mercantile system, is in the old 'City' of London, near the financial area and the river; Mr Tite Barnacle, Miss Wade, Mr Merdle, and the newly rich Mr Dorrit are all to be found well to the west in the fashionable Mayfair area; Mr Meagles, having left his bank, distances himself from the financial world by going up-river to Twickenham. The city is more than a vague background to the characters: through his use of settings, Dickens tells us about their lives and analyses the elements of an increasingly complex society (consider, for instance, Book 1, Chapter 14, 'Little Dorrit's Party'). (Some particularly topical aspects of the background to the novel are discussed below, in Part 3.)

The literary background

Men have been telling stories for centuries; but the dominant literary form of the nineteenth and twentieth centuries, the 'novel' as we generally understand the term—an extended piece of prose fiction—is a comparative newcomer to the hierarchy of the genres, having been established in English in the first half of the eighteenth century. When Dickens was born in 1812, Jane Austen (1775-1817), whose work he does not seem to have known, was at the height of her powers: *Pride and Prejudice* appeared in 1813, *Emma* in 1816. Sir Walter Scott (1771-1832) published in 1814 the first of the series of 'Waverley' novels which won him wealth and a European influence. But the account which Dickens left of his childhood reading (David gives a very similar account in Chapter 4 of *David Copperfield*) shows the importance to him of the eighteenth-century classics: Defoe (*Robinson Crusoe*, 1719); Fielding (*Tom Jones*, 1749); Smollett (*Roderick Random*, 1748, *Peregrine Pickle*, 1751, *Humphry Clinker*, 1771). He loved to impersonate his favourite characters in these works, which told, often within a rather loose structure, of the hero's adventures. From these novels, he learned some aspects of his early methods of construction, characterisation through exaggerated description and distinctive speech, and of plots including missing heirs, disguises, mistaken identities, and coincidental meetings. (You could consider how far these are elements of any Dickens novel you have read.) He did not, however, copy the sometimes thuggish and sexually promiscuous habits of many of their heroes; this is one of the changes that came about as the novel became a more 'respectable' form.

From the amount of reference in his novels, we can easily confirm his familiarity with the Bible, Shakespeare, and the marvellous oriental stories in the *Arabian Nights*; the literary tradition of Greece and Rome, on the other hand, meant much less to him. In Flora Finching's garbled sentimental speeches in *Little Dorrit*, we can see a wide range of literary sources, including recent Romantic poetry. Dickens's talents for accurate observation of physical appearance and gesture, combined with his ear for varieties of speech, had been cultivated during his early journalistic career, and were also of value in his amateur theatricals. The influence of popular theatre can be seen in some of his melodramatic plotting, and in his broad characterisation of comic or evil characters. Situations which in another novelist might be presented through the consciousness of a single character are often in Dickens presented dramatically, with the assumption that the reader knows how to interpret the psychological significance of what is described from the outside. One of Dickens's great strengths in widening and deepening the nature of his appeal to readers is his power of combining 'literary' elements in his work with those from more popular forms or derived from his direct observation of life. What holds them together is his increasing skill in planning their interaction as components of a single imaginative vision.

A note on the text

Dickens worked on *Little Dorrit* between January 1855 and May 1857. Following his usual practice, it was published by Bradbury and Evans in twenty parts in nineteen months (the last part being a double number) between December 1855 and June 1857. Each shilling number was accompanied by two etched illustrations by his regular collaborator Hablot K. Browne ('Phiz'). The completed novel, together with the Preface, was published in one volume by Bradbury and Evans in May 1857 at twenty-one shillings. (The artistic implications of serial publication are discussed below in 'The serialisation of *Little Dorrit*' in Part 3.)

There were various editions published in the author's lifetime, including the 'Charles Dickens' edition of 1868, in which the descriptive headlines found in many modern editions were added. There are various editions currently available, several of which reproduce some or all of the illustrations (though often reduced in scale and on paper which does not take the details well; it is worth looking in a library for an early edition). The Penguin edition, Penguin Books, Harmondsworth, 1967, has an introduction, notes, and map; the World's Classics edition, Oxford University Press, Oxford, 1982, adds Dickens's number plans, of great interest for tracing the construction of the novel. The standard scholarly edition (not for everyday use—it has no explanatory notes) is the Clarendon Dickens, Clarendon Press, Oxford, 1979, listed in Part 5 of these Notes.

Part 2

Summaries

of LITTLE DORRIT

A general summary

Little Dorrit is in part a mystery story, in which many incidents, motives and relationships between characters are not explained until near the end. For clarity, this summary anticipates some of that explanation.

Book the First: Poverty

Some forty years before the novel begins, old Gilbert Clennam compelled his timid nephew to marry a stern, bigoted, religious woman, who discovered that her husband had a child by a singer. Forcing a separation of the lovers, she brought up the child, Arthur Clennam, as her own son, and concealed old Gilbert's legacy to the singer (now dead) or to the youngest daughter or niece of her patron, Frederick Dorrit. The singer's papers had passed, via his twin-brother Ephraim, to Jeremiah Flintwinch, confidential servant to the now elderly and paralysed Mrs Clennam (later they are acquired by the criminal Rigaud, to blackmail her). Mr Clennam spent many years in China, and at the beginning of the novel, Arthur is returning to England after his death, with a sense of some wrong in the family's past waiting to be put right, but unaware of his true parentage.

On his way to England, Clennam passes through Marseilles (where the 'gentleman' Rigaud, awaiting trial for murder, lies in the same cell as the Italian Cavalletto) and meets Mr Meagles, a retired bank official, Mrs Meagles, their daughter Minnie ('Pet'), her companion, the foundling Harriet ('Tattycoram'), and the mysteriously distant Miss Wade. At his mother's gloomy London house, whose sights and sounds increasingly puzzle Flintwinch's wife Affery, he gets no reply to his questions, though unknown to him the young girl he meets there, Amy Dorrit, is the niece of Frederick, and therefore old Gilbert's legatee. Amy ('Little Dorrit') is the daughter of William, who has spent twenty years of genteel decay in the Marshalsea prison for debt, dependent on his loving daughter. Interested in the family through Amy, Clennam tries to pursue Mr Dorrit's case with the chief creditor, Mr Tite Barnacle, but quickly becomes the plaything of the Barnacle-dominated Circumlocution Office, where he again meets Mr Meagles, futilely pursuing the case of Daniel Doyce, an engineer-inventor, whose partner Clennam eventually becomes. Clennam visits Bleeding Heart Yard, where Doyce has his factory, and where Plornish the plasterer, a humble benefactor of Mr Dorrit, lives. The grasping landlord of the Yard turns out to be Casby ('The Patriarch'), a man of benevolent appearance, who squeezes the tenants through his agent, Pancks. Clennam is disillusioned to find Casby's daughter, his former sweetheart, now a middle-aged widow, Flora Finching, turned into a sentimental chatterbox. He is able to help Cavalletto, injured in the street, who has come to England in his flight from the sinister Rigaud, now acquitted of murder, whom he has met again in France.

While Clennam continues his interest in the self-sacrifice of Little Dorrit's work for her family, he finds himself drawn to Pet Meagles, who has, however, distressed her parents by welcoming the attentions of Henry Gowan, a gentleman-artist with Barnacle connections. Despite the pressure put on her by her father, Little Dorrit rejects the advances of John Chivery, son of the Marshalsea turnkey and another benefactor of her father. She accompanies her selfish sister Fanny to the home of Mrs Merdle, wife of a banker and politician on whom leaders of all branches of 'Society' fawn despite his mysterious unease. Mrs Merdle is buying Fanny off from an entanglement with Edmund Sparkler, her son by her first marriage.

Mr Meagles is now dealt a double blow by the defection of Tattycoram to the sinister Miss Wade, and by the engagement of Pet and Gowan. (Only the gratifying Barnacle connection gives Mr Meagles any consolation when the marriage duly takes place.) This also seems to mark the end of Clennam's hopes; in revealing this to Little Dorrit, he unwittingly gives her pain. (Rigaud, under one of his several aliases, meanwhile turns up with business to transact with Mrs Clennam.) Pancks, who has been taking a benevolent interest in the Dorrit family history, now reveals his discovery that Mr Dorrit is heir to a great estate; the long years of imprisonment end in a triumphal departure from the Marshalsea.

Book the Second: Riches

Some months later, the newly rich Dorrit family, on their way to Italy with the daughters' companion, Mrs General, spend the night at the convent of the Great St Bernard, along with Mr and Mrs Henry Gowan, and Rigaud (later revealed as Miss Wade's spy on the Gowans). Little Dorrit, unlike the rest of the family except for her uncle Frederick, is uneasy in the role her father's wealth requires of her, and lessens her isolation by her letters to Clennam; her snobbish father is impressed by the social positions of Gowan and of Mrs

Merdle, whom they also meet. Pet and Little Dorrit, both suspicious of Rigaud, are drawn closer together in the seemingly unreal atmosphere of Rome.

Clennam, still failing to understand the nature of Little Dorrit's feelings for him, continues to help Doyce. After Mr and Mrs Meagles leave for the Continent, he sees Tattycoram and Miss Wade meet Rigaud, and then visit Casby, who pays Miss Wade money from a trust. He is disturbed to find Rigaud also at his mother's house. Meanwhile Merdle, to further Sparkler's career in the Circumlocution Office, enlists the political influence of the Barnacles; public confidence in Merdle's financial schemes thus spreads, even in Bleeding Heart Yard, where Pancks tries to persuade Clennam to join him in investing.

In Rome, Fanny Dorrit, despite her sister's cautions, becomes engaged to Sparkler, to the pleasure of her socially conscious father, who, on their return to London, is delighted to have the acquaintance and investment advice of Mr Merdle. Returning to Italy with great plans, which may include marriage to Mrs General, Mr Dorrit disgraces himself at Mrs Merdle's dinner through a tragic delusion that he is still in prison. Once again dependent on Little Dorrit, he soon dies, followed by his brother Frederick.

Rigaud has mysteriously disappeared, leaving the house of Clennam under suspicion: Arthur visits Miss Wade and Tattycoram, who lead an unhappy life in Calais, but learns nothing useful. Miss Wade's written story of her life gives a distorted account of her 'torture' by people who have been kind to her, and of her deception by Henry Gowan (hence her tracking down of Pet, her use of Rigaud, and her taking up of Tattycoram). Doyce goes abroad to work, leaving his capital in the hands of Clennam, who eventually puts it into Merdle's schemes. He discovers that the missing Rigaud is the murderer from whom Cavalletto, now resident in the Yard, has fled; the Italian sets out in search of Rigaud/Blandois/Lagnier.

Mr Merdle, rumoured to be in line for a peerage, visits the Sparklers and borrows a penknife; he then goes to a bath-house and commits suicide, leaving a trail of forgery and robbery which will ruin thousands of investors and innocent bystanders. The crash thus involves Clennam, who is arrested for debt, ending up in Mr Dorrit's old room in the Marshalsea, where John Chivery reveals to him the secret of Little Dorrit's love, which he now recognises as the centre of his life, apparently lost for ever. After three months he is visited first by Rigaud, who has been hiding in order to put pressure on Mrs Clennam, and then by Little Dorrit, who brings him comfort and, what he will not accept, the offer of financial help. In a dramatic scene at the old house, in which both Mr and Mrs Flintwinch break out of their normal restraint, the mysteries in the Clennam family are clarified as Rigaud offers to sell Mrs Clennam the incriminating papers revealing the past, which will otherwise be read by Arthur. She passionately defends her role as God's instrument against sin but, released from her paralysis, rushes to the prison to promise restitution to Little Dorrit, the defrauded heiress, and to ask that the shameful story be concealed from Arthur. As Little Dorrit returns with her to appeal to Rigaud, they see the old house collapse, killing him; Mrs Clennam never moves or speaks again. (Flintwinch has meanwhile robbed the family firm.)

Pancks in his turn finally denounces Casby and exposes his hypocrisy by shearing the patriarchal locks in front of the Yard's dwellers. Clennam remains in prison while Mr Meagles scours the Continent for the originals of the missing documents; his return from his fruitless journey is immediately followed by the arrival of the repentant Tattycoram, bringing the papers left with Miss Wade by Rigaud. Meagles then brings back Doyce, a success abroad, who effects the prisoner's release. Little Dorrit, who has remained devoted to him, refuses to be separated from Clennam, especially now that there is no financial barrier to restrain him: all her father's money was lost in the Merdle crash. The threatening paper revealing the past is at her request burned unread by Clennam. Freed from prison and from the family shadow, he is at last sure of his destiny and marries Little Dorrit.

Detailed summaries

Preface to the 1857 edition

In this Preface to the first edition in book form, published immediately after the serialisation was complete, Dickens draws attention to his careful overall planning which drew the threads of the novel into a finished pattern. Defending the topical elements in the novel's social criticism, he appeals to common experience, but also draws attention to the recent mismanagement of the Crimean War and to large financial crashes due to fraud, some of which occurred during the writing of the novel. He describes his recent visit to the remains of the Marshalsea, where he saw the very part in which he had set much of the novel. Finally, he refers to the great success of the novel when serialised, and the importance to him of his reading public.

NOTES AND GLOSSARY:

Russian war . . . Court of Inquiry: Britain's war in the Crimea, 1854-6; a Committee of the House of Commons produced a damning report on the official conduct of the war (see 'The topical element' in Part 3).

Railroad-share epoch: mainly the 1840s, in which great fortunes were made, and several financial crashes occurred
a certain Irish bank: the Tipperary Bank, on which John Sadleir, MP, a former Junior Lord of the Treasury, brother of the manager, was overdrawn by £200,000; he committed suicide on 16 February 1856
Royal British Bank: its failure in 1856, through doubtful management conduct, had widespread repercussions, like Merdle's
Newton: Sir Isaac Newton (1642-1727), British scientist
Bleak House serialised 1852-3; like *Little Dorrit*, a long, complex novel involving mystery, coincidence, extensive patterns of symbolic imagery, and a selfless heroine; and constituting an attack on the inertia of British law and government

BOOK THE FIRST: POVERTY

Chapter 1: Sun and Shadow

In Marseilles, in the mid-1820s, on an August day of oppressive heat, Cavalletto, an Italian smuggler, and Rigaud, a 'cosmopolitan gentleman', are in prison. Rigaud, proud, sinister and dominating, is led out to be tried for the murder of his wife; the humble, though grotesque Cavalletto seems a more attractive character to the jailer's little daughter.

NOTES AND GLOSSARY:

builders of Babel: in the Bible, Genesis 11 tells how God scattered them on the earth, unable to understand each other's language, and therefore unable to complete the construction of the tower
Nice . . . Genoa . . .: places to the east of Marseilles in France, and on down the west coast of Italy
Rigaud: perhaps from French *rigolo,* joker
Death of my life!: Dickens renders literally various French phrases to remind us of Rigaud's origins
Exchange: place where financiers and others transact business

Chapter 2: Fellow Travellers

In Marseilles, the next day, Mr and Mrs Meagles and their attractive but over-dependent daughter Pet, newly returned from Egypt, are released from quarantine, as is Arthur Clennam, who is returning home after twenty years in China. Miss Wade, mysterious and aloof, overhears the passionate outburst of resentment of Pet's maid, Tattycoram, whom the Meagleses have taken from the Foundling Hospital.

NOTES AND GLOSSARY:

Allong and marshong: English pronunciation of words from the French revolutionary hymn, the *Marseillaise*

quarantine: isolation of travellers to avoid the spread of disease

Foundling Hospital: this institution was over eighty years old at the time of the action

Beadle: officer of a parish or civic institution (see Mr Bumble in Chapter 2 of *Oliver Twist*)

sanding: in order to absorb the wet ink

caravan: group of travellers, often of pilgrims, especially in the desert

Chapter 3: Home

On a dismal Sunday evening, Clennam returns to the grim, crooked London house where his paralysed mother nurses her vengeful religion, in a state of death-in-life, served by the old family retainer, Jeremiah Flintwinch, and his wife Affery. Clennam is reminded of the strain between his mother and his father (now dead) whose watch may contain a message to her. The presence of a girl, Little Dorrit, reminds him both of Pet Meagles and of his own lost sweetheart.

NOTES AND GLOSSARY:

Plague: the most famous London outbreak was the Great Plague of 1665

South Sea gods: at the time recent acquisitions of the great national collection

Calender's story: in the *Arabian Nights*, one of Dickens's favourite books

Arcadian: (*ironic*) pastoral, belonging to idealised countryside, as in ancient Greece

deadly sewer: the sewage-laden Thames, transmitting disease

Ludgate Hill: near St Paul's Cathedral

frock and drawers: children's clothing of the time

2 Ep. Thess. c.iii, v.6 &7: in this passage St Paul advises the faithful to shun the company of sinners

Worshipful Company: 'Livery' companies, based on crafts and trades, often had ancient meeting rooms

jack-towels . . .: a mocking description of stonework carved in traditional patterns

the Plagues of Egypt: punishments for sin, including flies and darkness, sent by God (see the Bible, Exodus 7)
watch-paper: a lining inside the case of a pocket-watch

Chapter 4: Mrs Flintwinch has a Dream

Flintwinch tries to convince Affery that it was in a nightmare that she saw him threaten his sleeping double and send him from the house with an iron box. (This is explained in Book 2, Chapter 30.)

NOTES AND GLOSSARY:
King Alfred the Great: believed to have invented a candle-clock
snuffers: device for trimming candles

Chapter 5: Family Affairs

Clennam withdraws from the family firm which is losing business, leaving his mother and Flintwinch in control. Mrs Clennam responds with religious self-righteousness to his suspicion that his father had wished to make reparation to someone injured by the firm. Though he leaves the house, he is increasingly interested in the unobtrusive, hard-working Little Dorrit, a young woman who seems like a child.

NOTES AND GLOSSARY:
consideration money: reward paid in cash

Chapter 6: The Father of the Marshalsea

More than twenty years before the time of the main action, William Dorrit was imprisoned in the Marshalsea for debts arising from a partnership. He has gradually resigned himself to a life in which, after the death of his wife, he has acquired a dubious status as a prisoner of long standing whose self-respect depends on petty snobbery. He has one son, Tip, and two daughters, Fanny and Amy (Little Dorrit, who was born in the prison).

NOTES AND GLOSSARY:
Southwark: 'the Borough', on the south side of the Thames
Marshalsea Prison: used for the imprisonment of debtors until shortly before Dickens wrote this novel (see 'The life of Charles Dickens' in Part 1)
gallipots: glazed pots, often used for medicine
paunch trade: trade in animal entrails as cheap food
three golden balls: a pawnbroker's shop sign

Father of the Marshalsea: perhaps on the analogy of 'Father of the House', for the longest-serving Member of Parliament ('Father' of course points to the irony of Dorrit's situation)

fustian: coarse cloth, marking the plasterer's low social status

Chapter 7: The Child of the Marshalsea

Little Dorrit's retiring behaviour arises from her divided life: she has taken on what should be her father's practical responsibilities for the family, and has acquired skills to earn money outside for him. While prison life has contaminated Tip, even Amy's innocence exists only in very unnatural circumstances she tries to conceal her prison life from the outside world.

NOTES AND GLOSSARY:

hard-bake: a sweetmeat, almond toffee (*Oxford English Dictionary*)

Palladium: place of safety (from the Greek goddess, Pallas Athene)

Clifford's Inn: north of the river, near the present-day Inns of Court

mock auction: Tip's job was to give a lead to real buyers

Chapter 8: The Lock

Clennam, following Little Dorrit home, is introduced to the Marshalsea by her uncle Frederick and discovers her self-sacrificing devotion to her sponging father. Locked overnight in the prison in error, he is engrossed in speculations about it, and wonders whether his mother's behaviour could be both self-punishment and an act of reparation to the Dorrit family for wrongs done to them.

NOTES AND GLOSSARY:

Levee: originally, morning reception held by the king

Camberwell: residential area further out from Southwark

Snuggery: private or select room, especially of a tavern

phaëton: a light, open horse carriage

Chapter 9: Little Mother

Clennam meets Little Dorrit by appointment and, hearing more of her family's situation, resolves to approach her father's most influential creditor, Mr Tite Barnacle of the Circumlocution Office, and also Mr Dorrit's friend, Plornish the plasterer. They meet Maggy, awkward and mentally retarded, who addresses Amy as 'Little Mother'. The narrator hints at the 'destined interweaving' of the stories of Clennam and Little Dorrit.

NOTES AND GLOSSARY:

Beau Nash: Richard Nash (*d*. 1762), master of ceremonies at Bath for fifty-six years

Grosvenor Square: in Mayfair, the fashionable West End

Bleeding Heart Yard: in contrast to the above, back in the older part of London, not far from St Paul's

Chapter 10: Containing the whole Science of Government

Pursuing Mr Dorrit's case, Clennam is fruitlessly passed to and fro between Barnacle in the Circumlocution Office and Barnacle at home, and recognises that the system has little to offer. He meets Mr Meagles, who is supporting the engineer and inventor, Daniel Doyce, another victim of the processes of the Office, whose factory is in Bleeding Heart Yard.

NOTES AND GLOSSARY:

Circumlocution Office: by mocking this imaginary office, Dickens attacks the British system of government (discussed in 'The topical element' in Part 3)

Gunpowder Plot: unsuccessful attempt to blow up Parliament in 1605, since commemorated annually on 5 November

jobbing . . . jobbed: from 'job', corrupt and selfish dealing (*colloquial*)

***its* name was Legion:** echoes an unclean spirit's answer to Jesus: 'for we are many' (see the Bible, Mark 5:9)

coach or crammer . . . below the bar: a civil servant sitting beyond the bar of the House of Commons to advise the government minister (this paragraph refers to various aspects of parliamentary procedure and language)

Barnacle: literally, a shellfish which hampers the ships it clings to (probably suggested by the old phrase 'Ship of State')

a sanguineous point of view: Tite Barnacle has married into an ancient 'patrician' but impoverished family

within the bills of mortality: living within a specific area which made reports on local deaths

Sir Thomas Lawrence: a fashionable painter (*d*. 1830)

Rats . . . Dog: sportsmen often made bets on the ability of dogs to kill rats
hocussed: drugged
memorialise: address a statement or memorandum to
nobs . . . snobs: (*slang*) the upper classes and those who wished to join their ranks
Newgate Calendar: records of notorious criminals, published at intervals after 1773

Chapter 11: Let Loose

A weary traveller, arriving at a French inn, overhears people expressing their hostility to Rigaud, who has been acquitted of murder, and himself turns out to be the ex-prisoner, posing as one Lagnier. By chance, he is to share a bedroom with his old acquaintance Cavalletto who, however, after agreeing to go to England, runs away.

NOTES AND GLOSSARY:

river Saone . . . Chalons: one hundred and fifty miles north of Marseilles
Cain: killer of his brother Abel, cursed by God as an outcast (see the Bible, Genesis 4)
diligence: a stage-coach
cabaret: tavern

Chapter 12: Bleeding Heart Yard

Clennam visits Bleeding Heart Yard, and employs Plornish to extricate Tip Dorrit from his debts and thus from prison. The plasterer's account of the struggles of the poor moves him to reflect on the insensitivity of the Circumlocution Office. We learn that Little Dorrit may first have been employed by Mrs Clennam through the Yard's landlord, Casby, 'an old acquaintance' of her son.

NOTES AND GLOSSARY:

tambour-worker: embroiderer of material on a circular frame
'Chaunter': (*slang*) fraudulent horse-seller (*Oxford English Dictionary*)
ten shillings in the pound: that is, the Plaintiff will settle for half of what he is owed, rather than get nothing at all
Wan: van: Dickens's London characters often interchange v and w: for other examples, see Plornish in Chapter 24, and the Wellers in *Pickwick Papers*

Chapter 13: Patriarchal

Clennam visits Casby, 'the Patriarch', a man of sharp business practice but vaguely beneficent appearance, which has aided him as agent for Lord Decimus Tite Barnacle. Casby in his turn works through his 'steam-tug', Pancks, a severely practical man. Confronted with his former beloved, Flora Casby, now the arch, voluble, middle-aged widow, Mrs Finching, Clennam is painfully disillusioned about the one romantic episode in his life. Later he is by chance able to help Cavalletto, recently arrived in London, whose leg was broken when he was knocked down by a coach. In his lodgings, Clennam's sorrowful musings about the value of his life are interrupted by the arrival of Little Dorrit.

NOTES AND GLOSSARY:

list shoes: slippers of coarse cloth (*Oxford English Dictionary*)

Patriarch: originally, the venerable head of an Israelite family

cross-cut: direct path between two points (*Oxford English Dictionary*)

Pagodian: Flora perhaps combines in a portmanteau word her notions of Chinese religion (Pagan) and architecture (Pagoda)

feet screwed back: Chinese girls' feet were bound up to restrict their growth

Paul and Virginia: in Bernardin de Saint-Pierre's (1737–1814) influential Rousseauist romance of the same name, published in 1787

post-chaises . . . to Scotland: to take advantage of the more liberal marriage laws

The Whole Duty of Man: an edifying religious work of the mid-seventeenth century

Smithfield . . . Barbican . . . Aldersgate Street: Clennam is walking south, towards St Paul's and the river

them Mails: mail-coaches

Chapter 14: Little Dorrit's Party

Little Dorrit, who appears to be a guardian to her father, sister, and Maggy, indirectly thanks Clennam for his help to her brother. Shut out of the prison for the first night in her life, she wanders with Maggy in the inhospitable streets of the 'great capital'. (She has come to wonder whether Flintwinch is spying on her.)

Chapter 15: Mrs Flintwinch has another Dream

Mrs Clennam's grim old house becomes increasingly mysterious to Affery, as she grows aware of strange noises and vibrations within it that contrast with its insulation from the outside world. She eavesdrops on a cryptic conversation between her mistress and her husband about Little Dorrit.

Chapter 16: Nobody's Weakness

On his way to visit the Meagles family, Clennam meets Daniel Doyce, and learns of his years of patient endeavour and need for a business partner. (Clennam decides to offer himself.) With some pain, he considers his possible attraction to the blooming Pet Meagles. She meanwhile is disturbed to learn that Tattycoram has met Miss Wade by appointment.

NOTES AND GLOSSARY:

Twickenham: more than a dozen miles upriver from central London (Fulham and Putney also lie by the river)

a look out: an object of desire (*Oxford English Dictionary*)

Corsair: a Mediterranean pirate (and the title of a work by Lord Byron (1788-1824) published in 1814)

the Fifth Commandment: the numbering varies between religious traditions, but that intended here is clearly the injunction to 'Honour thy father and thy mother' (see the Bible, Exodus 20)

rubber: that is, they played cards (bridge or whist)

Chapter 17: Nobody's Rival

Clennam is displeased to find that Pet delights in the presence of the unsuccessful gentleman-artist, Henry Gowan, to the evident distress of her parents, who are, however, snobbishly impressed by his connection with the Barnacle family. The change from fine to wet weather seems to mirror Clennam's emotions.

NOTES AND GLOSSARY:

Mount Etna: a volcano in Sicily

Kingston: several miles upstream from Twickenham, on the opposite bank

He won't set [Thames] on fire: traditional: he will not make much impact

Pall-Mall: fashionable London street, appropriate to 'saunter'

Palace at Hampton Court: still further upstream; favoured persons had free lodgings in the former royal residence
Claudes, Cuyps: that is, comparable with the paintings of the French and Dutch seventeenth-century masters
President and Council: of the Royal Academy, as experts in painting
Ecod: a mild oath

Chapter 18: Little Dorrit's Lover

John Chivery, the sentimental son of the turnkey of the Marshalsea, has ambitions of succeeding his father and of keeping Little Dorrit in the prison as his wife. Although aware of his good nature and his gifts to old Mr Dorrit, she is unwilling to consider him as her suitor.

NOTES AND GLOSSARY:
the ever young Archer: Cupid, god of love, son of Venus
glide down the stream of time: echoes Imlac in Ch. XXXV of Dr Johnson's (1709-84) *Rasselas* (1759)
Highlander: a figure in Highland dress was the traditional sign of a tobacconist's shop
slop-work: ready-made, cheap, or inferior garments (*Oxford English Dictionary*)

Chapter 19: The Father of the Marshalsea in two or three Relations

After patronising his feeble brother, Frederick, Mr Dorrit unsubtly reminds Amy of the practical value to him of her favourable response to Chivery's suit. From wallowing in self-pity at his decline in prison, he recovers to complacent self-deception about his role as father, while Little Dorrit comforts him, aware that she has never known his free self.

NOTES AND GLOSSARY:
classical daughter: she nourished her father in prison with her own milk
Lord Chesterfield: Lord Chesterfield (1694-1773) was the author of celebrated letters of guidance on conduct for his son

Chapter 20: Moving in Society

Further examples of Dorrit selfishness and pride are provided by Tip, now released, and by Fanny, whom Little Dorrit accompanies from the shabby world of the theatre to the opulence of Mrs Merdle's drawing-room. The wife of the great businessman buys off Fanny from a romantic entanglement with her son, Edmund Sparkler, on the grounds, repugnant to Miss Dorrit, that there is a social gulf between their families.

NOTES AND GLOSSARY:

'mugged': made faces, from 'mug'
Harley Street: north of Oxford Street, near Mayfair
Merdle: perhaps from French 'merde', excrement
powder: a footman in a formal powdered wig
Lo the poor Indian: 'Lo, the poor Indian, whose untutor'd mind Sees God in clouds, or hears him in the wind' (Alexander Pope (1688-1744), *An Essay on Man*, I.99-100; the poem was published in 1733)

Chapter 21: Mr Merdle's Complaint

At a reception in the Harley Street house, representatives of law, politics, religion, finance, and the armed forces offer the tribute of 'Society' to the rich and influential but curiously reticent Mr Merdle, who suffers from an undiagnosed complaint.

NOTES AND GLOSSARY:

hatchment: family shield displaying coat-of-arms outside the house of a dead person
Midas: Phrygian king who had the god-given powers mentioned here, but was later given ass's ears
Storr and Mortimer: a firm of jewellers
chuckle-headed: loutish
son-in-law: that is, stepson
Horse Guard magnates: officers of the sovereign's cavalry guard
Jack in the Green: a folk-figure dressed in bushy vegetation
Juno . . . Judith: Juno, the wife of the chief Roman god, Jupiter, was traditionally ample and stately; the biblical Book of Judith tells how the heroic widow killed the invader, Holofernes
root of all evil: properly, not money itself but the acquisitive attitude
amicus curiae: (*Latin*) as a friend of the court, disinterestedly
church presentations: right to nominate clergymen to fill offices
apron: part of bishop's attire
Achilles: Greek hero, invulnerable except in the heel by which his mother held him when she dipped him in the river Styx

Chapter 22: A Puzzle

Clennam finds disagreeable the idea that Little Dorrit might love John Chivery, and pities her distress at her father's situation.

NOTES AND GLOSSARY:

groves: Chivery's notion of the proper setting for his romantic melancholy

a pinting: Cockney pronunciation of 'pointing'

London Bridge . . . Iron Bridge: London Bridge was the busier, as it led to Borough High Street, Southwark

The George: an ancient Southwark inn

Chapter 23: Machinery in Motion

Clennam goes into partnership with Doyce in the factory in Bleeding Heart Yard, where he is visited by Flora Finching and her malignant relation by marriage, Mr F's Aunt. Flora's comic outpourings reveal a practical desire to help Little Dorrit. Pancks, though dealing grimly with the tenants in his professional capacity, also hopes to help her.

NOTES AND GLOSSARY:

Abel's murder: by Cain (see note on Chapter 11)

oft in the stilly night: first line of a lyric by the Irish poet Thomas Moore (1779-1852)

severed the golden bowl—I mean bond: a muddled reminiscence of the Bible, Ecclesiastes 12:6, 'Or ever the silver cord be loosed, or the golden bowl be broken'

oil of something: to poison himself

humbug of a thousand guns: warships were rated by the number of guns they carried

Chapter 24: Fortune-telling

Little Dorrit accepts Flora's kindly offer of work, and is partly paid in romantic confidences about Clennam's past. Despite the mysterious benevolent interest of Pancks in her family, she becomes even more retiring. She tells Maggy the story of the little woman who patiently guarded the shadow of a good man until her death.

NOTES AND GLOSSARY:

mahogany: that is, deeply tanned

man in the iron mask: a mysterious French prisoner in later seventeenth century, whose identity was never discovered

the Spartan boy: an example of silence and fortitude under stress

at score: at full speed, suddenly (*Oxford English Dictionary*)

'You must know . . . ': in this outpouring, Flora appears to cross references to the mark of Cain (see the Bible, Genesis 4), the Pygmalion story inverted, the end of Shakespeare's (1564-1616) *The Winter's Tale*, and Wordsworth's (1770-1850) *Prelude*, XI,107-9: 'Bliss was it in that dawn to be alive'

fifth of November: that is, carried through the streets like the effigy of Guy Fawkes (see note on 'Gunpowder Plot', Chapter 10)

laid up in ordinary: (*nautical*) out of commission (*Oxford English Dictionary*)

grubber: one who gets together wealth by sordid or contemptible methods; compare 'money-grubber'

Chapter 25: Conspirators and Others

Pancks employs his landlord, Mr Rugg, and John Chivery in his enquiries about the Dorrits. Cavalletto's cheerful character gradually wears down the insular prejudices of Bleeding Heart Yard.

NOTES AND GLOSSARY:

Pentonville: north-west of St Paul's, near today's King's Cross area

pining shepherd: more fun at Chivery's poetic self-dramatisation

ambrosial: divine (ambrosia: the food of the gods)

flour-dredger . . . coffee-biggin: box with holes in lid, for sprinkling flour; a patent coffee pot

Chapter 26: Nobody's State of Mind

Despite his own good intentions, Clennam increasingly dislikes Henry Gowan, but agrees to visit his mother at Hampton Court Palace where, in addition to discovering the class of genteel parasites, he begins to feel uncertain about the Gowans' intentions towards Pet Meagles.

NOTES AND GLOSSARY:

Bank of England . . . London Wall: just to the north-east of St Paul's

Bohemians: extends the idea of 'civilised gipsies'

had his own crow to pluck: his own dispute to settle

écarté: a card game, involving 'discarding' from one's hand (compare Miss Wade's story in Book 2, Chapter 21)

Chapter 27: Five-and-Twenty

As Clennam rededicates himself to practical duty, he is asked by Mr Meagles to assist in the recovery of Tattycoram, who has left in an outburst of resentment. They find her with Miss Wade, whose sinister influence encourages her passionate rejection of the alleged condescension with which the Meagles family had treated her.

NOTES AND GLOSSARY:

Strait was the gate . . . motes from other men's eyes: echoes of Christ's Sermon on the Mount (see the Bible, Matthew 7), the second a warning against hypocrisy

Grosvenor region: in Mayfair, evidently not far from Mr Tite Barnacle's (Chapter 10)

dunghills in the Mews: because the carriage-horses were stabled there

caravanserai: enclosed court where the caravans stop for rest

Chapter 28: Nobody's Disappearance

Clennam arrives on a calm evening at the Meagles cottage to discover that Pet and Henry Gowan are engaged, to the grief of her parents. Despite his brave face, Clennam seems to be saying farewell to his own hopes.

Chapter 29: Mrs Flintwinch goes on Dreaming

Affery's confusion increases as her husband continues his strange behaviour. Pancks carries his enquiries about Little Dorrit into their household, and Mrs Clennam reveals unsuspected gentleness in her dealings with the girl. On an ominously thundery evening, Affery is confronted by a mysterious, newly arrived foreigner (recognisable to the reader as Rigaud).

NOTES AND GLOSSARY:

Custom House . . .: near the north (City) side of London Bridge

Chapter 30: The Word of a Gentleman

Rigaud, now passing as Blandois, initially seems to recognise Mr Flintwinch (his mistake is explained in Book 2, Chapter 30). In his character of 'gentleman', he has business to transact with the Clennam firm, and is particularly interested in the letters 'D.N.F.' (Do Not Forget) in the lining of the dead husband's watch, which leads

Mrs Clennam to justify her grim mode of life. Rigaud then apparently returns to France.

Chapter 31: Spirit

Mrs Plornish's pauper father, Old Nandy, the object of cheap patronage by Mr Dorrit, is the touchstone by which the true charity of Little Dorrit and the selfish pretensions of Fanny and her father are revealed. Tip insults Clennam for his earlier refusal of a 'loan'.

NOTES AND GLOSSARY:

Workhouse . . . law . . . Good Samaritan . . . twopence: there is an evident contrast between the harshness of the formal institution and the spirit of the Gospel parable (see the Bible, Luke 10)

Lord Chancellor: Speaker of the House of Lords, head of legal system

Lord Chamberlain: officer of the royal household

Chloe, Phyllis, Strephon: names traditional in poetry since Classical Greece, here indicating a debased tradition

pollard: cropped (more usual of trees or animals)

vassalage: state of dependence

going over the water: across the Thames, to the Marshalsea

the bruised reed: Mr Dorrit quotes from God's words in the Bible, Isaiah 42:3

a livery: garb indicating Nandy's pauper status

Chapter 32: More Fortune-Telling

In his anxiety to promote Little Dorrit's welfare, Clennam unwittingly gives her pain by revealing his resignation to a solitary life after the loss of Pet, and showing no recognition of Little Dorrit's love for him. Pancks is clearly on the point of making some momentous revelation to the family.

NOTES AND GLOSSARY:

in blue water . . . among the heather: echoes or parodies of popular songs

Pipes in faggots: in bundles, plentifully

Pedigree: chart of the Dorrit ancestry

Chapter 33: Mrs Merdle's Complaint

Mrs Gowan receives, through Mrs Merdle, Society's blessing on the fictions attached to her son's forthcoming marriage, in which financial considerations play a crucial part. Mrs Merdle points out to her husband that he, dully absorbed in his affairs, seems vulgar to the fashionable world sustained at his expense. His unease continues.

NOTES AND GLOSSARY:

Job: Mrs Gowan plainly lacks his famed resignation, related in the biblical Book of Job

to have and to hold: from the marriage service, and not lawyers' language as Mrs Gowan suggests

to coin money: (*colloquial*) make money quickly; it also hints at Mr Merdle's forgery

parable of the camel: in the Bible Jesus says (Mark 10: 25) 'It is easier for a camel to go through the eye of a needle, than for a rich man to enter into the Kingdom of God'

Chapter 34: A Shoal of Barnacles

Clennam remains uneasy as to Gowan's being worthy of Pet, but attends the marriage, which is dominated by Barnacle relatives, the only point of gratification to Mr Meagles.

NOTES AND GLOSSARY:

despatch-box: for holding official papers

Prospero: the magician in Shakespeare's *The Tempest*

pass the bottle of smoke: pass the oriental hookah pipe (suggesting acceptance of a social role)

Quarter Days: four set days of the year on which money fell due for payment

private loaf and fish trade: a glance at Jesus's miracle in feeding five thousand people (see the Bible, Matthew 14)

Speaker: presiding officer of the House of Commons

places: government posts

the Flying Dutchman: (*legendary*) a sea-captain doomed to sail endlessly until the Day of Judgment

John Bull: the symbol of a typical Englishman, described by John Arbuthnot (1667-1735) in 1712 (compare the American 'Uncle Sam')

Chapter 35: What was behind Mr Pancks on Little Dorrit's Hand

Pancks reveals to Clennam how at his own expense he has conducted a lengthy investigation to prove Mr Dorrit heir to a great unclaimed estate. Arthur breaks the news to Little Dorrit, who is concerned solely for her father's welfare. The pathos of Mr Dorrit's reaction to the news is mingled with his snobbery in a desire to live up to his new status. His daughter cannot understand why, after so much suffering, he should still have to pay his debts.

NOTES AND GLOSSARY:

Common Pleas: the Court in which her lawsuit (Chapter 25) was heard

'tis distance lends . . . : from Thomas Campbell's (1777-1844) *Pleasures of Hope* (1799)

Woodpecker Tapping: another lyric by Thomas Moore

smelling-bottles: bottles containing salts to dispel faintness

Chapter 36: The Marshalsea becomes an Orphan

Like Tip and Fanny, Mr Dorrit adopts something of the grand manner in his new-found fortune, convinced that he has a position to fill, though he cannot totally conceal his vulnerable humanity. The departure from the Marshalsea is a public event, marred only by the exit of Little Dorrit, carried out insensible and in her old, shabby clothes, by Clennam.

NOTES AND GLOSSARY:

cabriolet: light carriage

chariot: pleasure carriage

his dinners . . . at six: dining in the evening, rather than in the middle of the day, was, and still is, an upper-class custom

bumper: a glass filled to the brim

fettered African: a slave, making an appeal to the common element in all humanity

Sir Roger de Coverley: a famous character invented in the *Spectator* essays (essay No. 112 is referred to here) of Joseph Addison (*d.* 1719)

bundled up the steps: folded them up to the carriage body

BOOK THE SECOND: RICHES

Chapter 1: Fellow Travellers

On an autumn evening, various groups of travellers on their way from France to Italy arrive at the convent of the Great St Bernard for shelter. Although the names are not revealed until the end of the chapter, we recognise Mr Dorrit, travelling with his family and retinue of servants; Henry Gowan and the former Pet Meagles (to whom Little Dorrit gives a message from Clennam); and Rigaud, still passing as Blandois.

NOTES AND GLOSSARY:

another Ark: Genesis 6 tells how God commanded Noah to make the original Ark, to escape from the universal flood

grated house: that is, the mortuary, with an iron grille

fourgon: luggage wagon

famous dogs: the breed, which still survives, was used to rescue travellers from the snow

Chapter 2: Mrs General

Among the Dorrit suite is Mrs General, paid chaperone to the daughters, a middle-aged lady devoted to the proprieties, and to avoiding the recognition of anything unpleasant in life.

NOTES AND GLOSSARY:

black velvet housings: funeral trappings on the horses

the late service: the Burial of the Dead, which is echoed in the following words

phoenix: model of excellence (the unique bird of fable regularly arose rejuvenated from its own ashes)

Herculaneum: below the volcano of Vesuvius, near Naples in Italy, visited by Dickens in 1845

Chapter 3: On the Road

Little Dorrit's solicitude for Pet Gowan offends against the characteristic Dorrit horror of any reminder of their 'low' state (hence the distortion of their relationship with Clennam). She also seems alone in finding something sinister about Blandois. Arriving at a hotel, the travellers find Mrs Merdle (who conceals her acquaintance with Fanny) and Sparkler (who cannot). The journey to Italy and the stay in Venice serve to isolate Little Dorrit from her family, as they adopt new roles in a world of 'misery and magnificence', while for her the world of the Marshalsea is the only reality; all else is a dream.

NOTES AND GLOSSARY:

puppy: conceited or impertinent young man

Simplon: pass from Switzerland to northern Italy

Chapter 4: A Letter from Little Dorrit

Little Dorrit writes from Venice to reassure Clennam about Pet's welfare, though she has her doubts about Gowan. In Italy, she is still mentally in London, unable to reform herself according to Mrs General's methods, and aware that her desire to express directly her love for her father is an offence against propriety. She still regards herself, as she hopes he will, as Clennam's 'poor child', 'the little shabby girl', and signs her letter 'Little Dorrit'.

Chapter 5: Something Wrong Somewhere

Mr Dorrit causes grief to Amy by rebuking her, with Mrs General's aid, for failing to blot out the effects of the 'accursed' Marshalsea experience; her awareness of the shadow in his life causes her to pity rather than reproach him. She has drawn closer to her uncle Frederick, who does not entirely share the family attitudes. In a discussion of whether they should keep up their acquaintance with the Gowans, Mr Dorrit is decisively influenced in their favour by the connection with the national benefactor, Mr Merdle. Frederick, in an extraordinary outburst, denounces the family pretensions, particularly as they give pain to Amy.

NOTES AND GLOSSARY:

hoodwinked: covered up from sight (*Oxford English Dictionary*)
Rialto: the Exchange quarter of Venice
Act of Parliament: Fanny's joke refers to the elaborate procedure then necessary to dissolve a marriage

Chapter 6: Something Right Somewhere

Gowan, rootless and cynical, has taken up with Blandois, partly to assert his independence of his wife. When the Dorrit sisters pay their visit, he is painting Blandois, who he suggests might be angel, devil or murderer. Gowan's cruelty to his dog which seems naturally hostile to Blandois, arouses Little Dorrit's fear of his insensitivity to his wife. (The dog is mysteriously poisoned.) Mr Sparkler is now taken up, with different degrees of self-knowledge, by Mr Dorrit and Fanny, whose conduct seems shallow to Amy.

NOTES AND GLOSSARY:

pre-Adamite: ancient
bravo: a hired assassin ('Monk' Lewis (*d.* 1818) wrote a romance, *The Bravo of Venice*)
common enemy: of mankind: Satan
Cattivo Soggetto Mio: (*Italian*) my wicked fellow (Blandois is also the painter's 'subject')
gaby: simpleton

Old File: someone sharp or cunning
leaves round his head: the poet's laurel crown
the City: (of London) the centre of the financial world
like Venus's son: Cupid (see Book 1, Chapter 18); Aphrodite, the Greek equivalent of Venus, rose from the sea
Doges: chief magistrates of Venice until the Napoleonic conquest

Chapter 7: Mostly, Prunes and Prism

Little Dorrit is surprised by Fanny's opinion that their father will soon fall victim to the marital designs of Mrs General. The 'Prunes and Prism' school of behaviour notwithstanding, Amy and Pet are drawn closer together by their repugnance at the lurking presence of Blandois, the probable killer of the dog. To Little Dorrit, the whole tourist existence resembles the Marshalsea, with travellers in the custody of guides, without the power to organise their own lives; even in Rome, where they again meet Mrs Merdle, a leader of its society, she finds only artificiality and second-hand experience.

NOTES AND GLOSSARY:
Maecenas: in first century BC rich patron of the Latin poets Horace (65-8 BC) and Virgil (70-19 BC)
sizar: a college student with an allowance
Corso: a main thoroughfare in Rome, near the Classical antiquities

Chapter 8: The Dowager Mrs Gowan is reminded that 'It Never Does'

In contrast to the leisured tourists, Doyce and Clennam are successfully devoting themselves to productive work; Clennam even takes up once again the cause of his partner's invention with the Circumlocution Office. Little Dorrit's letter from Venice reminds him of his loss which, unaware of the nature of her feelings, he continues to see as that of a child. Mrs Gowan meanwhile severs her relationship with the Meagleses by insisting on her false account of the circumstances leading up to their children's marriage.

NOTES AND GLOSSARY:
Bedlamite: a lunatic (from Bethlehem Royal Hospital)
red tape: here, literally: tape used on government papers
from Hyde Park Corner to the General Post Office: from the fashionable West End to the City of London
ambuscade of green fan: recalls her earlier bushy appearance

Chapter 9: Appearance and Disappearance

Mr and Mrs Meagles leave for the Continent to visit the Gowans. Clennam, seeing by chance Tattycoram in the street with a mysterious stranger (recognisable to the reader as Rigaud/Blandois), watches them meet Miss Wade by the river. Following them, he is surprised to find them visit Mr Casby; but when Arthur is admitted to the Patriarch's presence, he gets no useful information from him; in conversation with Pancks, however, he deduces that some of the trust money which Casby regularly pays Miss Wade is to be given to the stranger. (This is explained in Book 2, Chapter 28.) Pancks (who regards Miss Wade as tortured and dangerous) reveals his own temptation to 'do for' his proprietor.

NOTES AND GLOSSARY:

the Adelphi: a terrace (now gone) built by Robert Adam in later eighteenth century

crossed the Strand: they go north, away from the river

the great building: Coram's Foundling Hospital (see Book 1, Chapter 2)

dying gladiators and Belvederes: references to two famous classical sculptures in Rome; the 'Belvedere' is a statue of Apollo

Venice Preserved: a tragedy (1682) by Thomas Otway (1652-85)

Mantua . . . Mantua-making: one a town in Italy, the other from the French 'manteau', a loose robe

pelerine: a long narrow cape (*Oxford English Dictionary*)

Chapter 10: The Dreams of Mrs Flintwinch thicken

In an interval between attendances at the Circumlocution Office, Clennam visits his mother's dark house, where he now meets Blandois face to face, with some hostility. Although he leaves them to their business, he is aware of some oddness in his mother's behaviour.

NOTES AND GLOSSARY:

broken alive on that wheel: an ancient method of torture

teetotum: small spinning-top

bagwig: wig with a bag at the back of head to hold hair

Chapter 11: A Letter from Little Dorrit

Little Dorrit again writes to Clennam, giving news of Rome. The Gowans are in rather shabby lodgings while Henry, whom she suspects of being a hollow man, paints her father. His loyal wife has recently had a son, after the arrival of her parents. Gowan's mysterious friend is at present away. (The reader knows that Clennam has met him in London.) Little Dorrit herself thinks often of home, of the beloved scene of her poverty and Clennam's kindness, and dreams of herself as a poor child, embarrassingly revealing the family past.

Chapter 12: In which a Great Patriotic Conference is holden

As the idolisation of Merdle increases (which casts doubts on the sagacity or honesty of his acquaintance), he gives a dinner to enlist the political influence of the Barnacles in furthering the career of Edmund Sparkler, who soon becomes one of the 'Lords of the Circumlocution Office'. Thus government support increases the financial success of Merdle. (With some difficulty the Office has accepted Mr Dorrit's payment of his debt.)

NOTES AND GLOSSARY:

basilisk: fabulous creature with death-dealing eyes

Whittington: Richard Whittington, a fifteenth-century Mayor of London and public benefactor

one Mood, the Imperative: that is, Mrs Merdle is commanding her husband

Colossus: in Classical times, a huge statue at entry of Rhodes harbour

***in Banco*:** (*Latin*) on the bench, in court

Captain Macheath: highwayman-hero of John Gay's (1685-1732) *The Beggar's Opera*(1728), a satire on corruption in high places

Tyburn Tree: the gallows, where Marble Arch now stands

Westminster Hall: seat of chief law courts until 1882

seven-league dress-shoes: a variant on the 'boots' of fairy tale

lobby: entrance hall to Houses of Parliament

Dr Johnson's . . . acquaintance: see James Boswell's (1740-95) *Life of Johnson*, under 1770; the joke was repeated in Benjamin Disraeli's (1804-81) novel, *Sybil* (1845)

dame's house: public-school lodging kept by a woman

Parliamentary pairs: members in opposite parties who agree to be absent at the same time

interest: personal or political influence

Mr Merdle's pocket: in a 'pocket borough' one man could control the election of an MP

detainers: legal warrants

Buhl tables: inlaid with brass (from C. A. Boulle, *d.* 1732)

Chapter 13: The Progress of an Epidemic

In Bleeding Heart Yard, Mrs Plornish has set up shop, assisted by Mr Dorrit's money; Cavalletto behaves strangely after seeing an evil man of whom he is afraid (that is, Rigaud). Belief in the power of Merdle has spread like an infection, touching Cavalletto and even the practical Pancks, who has invested his thousand pounds and tries to persuade Clennam to do likewise, to provide capital to back Daniel Doyce, and perhaps to remedy the wrongs he fears in his own family past. Gradually Clennam begins to doubt his own instinctive distrust of Merdle.

NOTES AND GLOSSARY:

crack end: that is, 'cracked-up', superior

Pastoral . . . Golden Age: literary form celebrating the legendary time of innocence and harmony

Chapter 14: Taking Advice

Following Sparkler's elevation, Fanny Dorrit, despite her sister's cautions about the necessity of love and devotion, becomes engaged to him, partly as a gesture of independence and partly as an act against Mrs Merdle.

NOTES AND GLOSSARY:

Tiber: river by which Rome stands

sinecure: paid post involving little or no work

Gate of the People . . . Albano: the northern entrance; a town to the south

a flat sister: a sister lacking in spirit

a cat in gloves: such a cat proverbially fails to catch mice

mother-in-lawed: that is, step-mothered

Chapter 15: No Just Cause or Impediment why these Two Persons should not be joined together

After Mrs Merdle and Mr Dorrit spar about the practical arrangements concerning the marriage, which takes place before Sparkler returns to his post, Fanny asserts herself against the rule of Mrs General. Mr Dorrit again seems selfish, money-conscious and, in his desire that she too should make a 'worthy' marriage, insensitive to Amy, who, left very much alone after Fanny's marriage, takes to wandering in the ruins of old Rome and reminders of the ruins in her own life.

NOTES AND GLOSSARY:

Chapter title: words from the marriage service
Seven Hills: on which Rome was built
Marplot: a character in Mrs Centlivre's (1667-1723) play *The Busybody* (1708) who hinders designs despite good intentions
Beggar's Petition: that is, the customs officers all asked for bribes
ancient Belisarius: a Roman general who became a beggar
Romulus: mythical founder of Rome
myrmidons: troop, originally of Achilles's men in the Trojan War
She-Wolf: a she-wolf suckled Romulus and his brother Remus
Capitol: the Temple of Jupiter, on the Capitoline Hill
Emperors of the Soldiery: in the third century AD, support from the army was the basis of rule
Vesta: the Roman goddess of domestic life
Slough of Despond: in the allegory of John Bunyan's (1628-88) *Pilgrim's Progress* (1678), a mental state represented by the difficult terrain

Chapter 16: Getting on

The newly married Sparklers come to lodge in London with Mr Merdle. More importantly, the great man visits Mr Dorrit and does him public honour, thereby inducing Society to follow. Stressing the importance of integrity in business, he also offers him investment opportunities. To Mr Dorrit, the reflected glory is like a golden dream, marred only by the severe scrutiny of the Harley Street butler.

NOTES AND GLOSSARY:

popular conception of Guy Fawkes: a stuffed effigy without hands
revised the New Testament: see note on Book 1, Chapter 33
track of the Apostle: St Peter (see the Bible, Acts 5:15)
dust-cart: for human excrement as well as ashes (compare 'Merdle')
golden Street of the Lombards: Lombard Street, at the heart of the financial area
auriferously: in a manner which yielded gold

Chapter 17: Missing

Mr Dorrit is visited by Flora Finching in the hope that, as a traveller from Italy, he may know something of the mysterious disappearance of

Blandois after leaving Mrs Clennam's, which seems to leave the family under suspicion. Hoping to carry information about his friend back to Gowan in Italy, Mr Dorrit visits Mrs Clennam, who suggests that Blandois may be in hiding. The household, and the mysterious rustling noises which terrify Mrs Flintwinch, combine to disturb the enquirer's peace.

NOTES AND GLOSSARY:

college Bachelor: Bachelor of Arts and not, as Flora thinks, an unmarried man
solus: (*Latin*) alone
rusty screw: ill-tempered, miserly person (*Oxford English Dictionary*)
Temple Bar, headless: Temple Bar stood in Fleet Street, as gateway to the City of London; heads of traitors were formerly exhibited on spikes
in the Commission of the Peace: a Justice, magistrate

Chapter 18: A Castle in the Air

Before leaving for the Continent, Mr Dorrit is visited by John Chivery, whose kindness is only recognised when he is seen not to have come as an insulting reminder of the Marshalsea (whose inmates benefit by a cheque for a hundred pounds). On the road through France and Italy, Mr Dorrit indulges in grandiose plans which seem to include Mrs General.

NOTES AND GLOSSARY:

Miss Biffin: a limbless fairground show
castle-building: indulging in ill-founded dreams (see Chapter 19)
Le Brun: a seventeenth-century French painter and author
Saone . . . Rhone: French rivers flowing south
Cornice road: road running east along the coast
Civita Vecchia: a town some thirty miles north of Rome

Chapter 19: The Storming of the Castle in the Air

Before entering Rome, Mr Dorrit meets a funeral procession. At home, he initially seems jealous of his brother's closeness to Amy, and attributes to him all his own physical and mental weaknesses. For the first time since his liberation, Little Dorrit serves her father as she had done in the Marshalsea, which increasingly shadows his mind. (He is, however, able to introduce to Mrs General the subject of their future relationship.) At Mrs Merdle's select dinner, he mortifies her by reverting completely to his prison ways and revealing his family's past; at home he returns to complete dependence on Little Dorrit, trying to pawn his jewellery. After ten days he dies, his face at last freed from prison influence to become younger than she has ever seen it. His brother Frederick, faithful to the last, accompanies him even in death.

NOTES AND GLOSSARY:

rumble: outside seat at the back of the carriage

Goths reversed: bringing luxuries, unlike the savage tribes who sacked Rome in 410 AD

Chapter 20: Introduces the next

Clennam, having learned of Miss Wade's whereabouts from Pancks's search in Casby's papers, gains admittance to her Calais lodgings by a subterfuge, in the hope that she will give information about Blandois which will clear the house of Clennam of any responsibility for his disappearance. Miss Wade, who has used the man as a paid agent, has nothing to impart, but directs suspicion back to Mrs Clennam. She and Tattycoram (now known again as Harriet) lead a restless existence of mutual torture; and in order to explain the nature of her hate for Gowan and his wife, she has already written for Clennam an account of her life.

NOTES AND GLOSSARY:

packet: the regular ship on the Channel run

Chapter 21: The History of a Self-Tormentor

Miss Wade's paper, which insists on her clear-sightedness, tells of her upbringing as an orphan, the affection and kindness of children and adults, which she 'saw' as mere insulting patronage, and her employment as a governess, which she interprets as emotional self-indulgence by her mistress. Despite her passionate attachments, she has never trusted where she has loved: even when engaged, with every prospect of fortune, she has proudly resented her fiancé. Only his friend, Henry Gowan, seemed to understand her and encourage her contempt; but when she broke her engagement she discovered that Gowan too had merely trifled with her, and was courting Pet Meagles. Hatred arising from this caused Miss Wade to travel, until she met Pet in Marseilles (in Chapter 2); there she also took up Tattycoram, recognising a fellow rebel against what she too sees as condescending patronage. She has, however, failed to release her from her 'bondage and sense of injustice'.

NOTES AND GLOSSARY:

easy with: ambiguous, as the conversation shows: (1) at ease with; (2) equal to

dressed-up Death: in the illustrations of the Dance of Death, in which Death touched people of all groups

anatomise: lay bare people's characters

breaking mere house-flies on the wheel: see note on Book 2, Chapter 10; here, perhaps an echo of Pope's *Epistle to Dr Arbuthnot* (1735), l.308: 'who breaks a butterfly upon a wheel?'

in her society: in Marseilles, in Book 1, Chapter 2

Chapter 22: Who passes by this Road so late?

Daniel Doyce goes abroad to work for a government more receptive to practical achievement, leaving his invention and the management of his capital to Clennam, who calls on the testimony of Pancks to dispel Doyce's prejudice against financial speculation. In the factory, Clennam discovers that the Blandois who overshadows his mother's house is identical with the assassin from whom Cavalletto has fled. To resolve the mystery, the Italian sets out in search of Blandois.

NOTES AND GLOSSARY:

Power . . . barbaric one: only as seen from the Circumlocution Office

plastic . . . thumb: able to mould or create

Chapter 23: Mistress Affery makes a Conditional Promise, respecting her Dreams

Clennam surprises his mother with the news of Blandois' past, but can prise no revelation from her. In an attempt to gain an interview with Mrs Flintwinch, he tours the house with Flora Finching, who interprets this as a romantic subterfuge. While Cavalletto, unknown to Arthur (see Book 2, Chapter 30), detains her husband with questions about Blandois, Affery will only reveal that the house is full of whisperings and noises.

NOTES AND GLOSSARY:

brazen wall: echoes the Bible, Jeremiah 15:20

old fabled influence: of Medusa, one of the three Gorgons of Classical legend

phosphorus-box: box containing matches tipped with chlorate of potash with phosphorus on which to ignite them (*Oxford English Dictionary*)

allegorical personage: Britannia, for instance, is represented holding a trident
mantling in: suffusing with blood
Take care how you judge others: 'Judge not, that ye be not judged': see the Bible, Matthew 7:1
well-known spectre: an optical illusion on the Brocken peak in Saxony, caused by a magnified projection of shadows

Chapter 24: The Evening of a Long Day

On a tedious Sunday evening, Fanny Sparkler is thinking selfishly of the recent deaths in the Dorrit family but recognises Amy's devotion in looking after Tip in his subsequent illness. Unusually, Mr Merdle, rumoured to be destined for a peerage, pays a casual visit; he has typically little to say, but intends to 'go by the shortest way'; as he leaves, he borrows a dark-handled penknife.

NOTES AND GLOSSARY:
baronetcy: lowest hereditary title, not carrying a seat in the House of Lords
the old scythe: of Father Time
aromatic vinegar: to dispel 'the vapours'
Quinbus Flestrin: the name the tiny Lilliputians give Gulliver in Book 1 of *Gulliver's Travels* (1726) by Jonathan Swift (1667-1745)
situation . . . disqualifies me: Fanny is pregnant, hence the remark about her 'figure'
Yellow Jack: yellow fever
little Twoshoes: character in an eighteenth-century nursery story
tile: (*slang*) a tall hat
ink it: stain it while trimming the tip of a quill pen
Chelsea Pensioner or Greenwich Veteran: residents in the foundations for ex-servicemen (here suggesting mutilation in war)

Chapter 25: The Chief Butler Resigns the Seals of Office

Mr Merdle fails to accompany his wife to dinner with Physician, who is called out later that night to find that the financier has committed suicide with Fanny's knife at a bath-house. The Chief Butler pronounces his employer no gentleman, and resigns. After a period of sympathetic rumour, the catastrophic truth of Merdle's forgery and robbery produces the revelation of his having been known as low and reckless; the crash will blight the lives of thousands.

NOTES AND GLOSSARY:

Seals of Office: normally held by an appointee of the Crown or an official body

on his own trumpet: sounding his own praises

Term: the months during which the law courts are open

default: here, Mr Merdle's failure to come to dinner, but anticipating the revelations about his business

Banquo's chair: see Shakespeare's *Macbeth*, III.4: vacant because Banquo has been murdered; his ghost appears to the King

sarcophagus: stone coffin

laudanum: a common drug of the period: tincture of opium

busy bee . . . shining hours: 'How doth the little busy bee/Improve each shining hour,/And gather honey all the day/ From every opening flower!' From Isaac Watts's (1674-1748) *Divine Songs for Children,* XX

High 'Change: high point of business on the Exchange

Dome of St. Paul's: apart from the symbolic value of the church, relevant for its proximity to the financial area

roc's egg: a great prize (roc: a fabulous bird in the *Arabian Nights*)

new constellation . . . wise men: (*ironic*) the magi followed a star to find Jesus in the stable at Bethlehem (see the Bible, Matthew 2)

Chapter 26: Reaping the Whirlwind

Merdle's crash swallows up all Doyce's money, which Clennam has invested. To clear Doyce's name, Clennam honourably takes all the public odium on himself and is arrested for debt. Choosing to go to the Marshalsea, he is put by John Chivery in the room full of memories, once occupied by William Dorrit.

NOTES AND GLOSSARY:

Chapter title: see the Bible, Hosea 8:7: 'For they have sown the wind, and they shall reap the whirlwind'

model structures of straw: compare Mr Dorrit's Castle in the Air (Book 2, Chapter 19)

Palace Court: the Marshalsea Court

caption: an arrest

King's Bench: court which sent debtors to a prison close by the Marshalsea

tyfling madder: conventional representation of speech of English Jews

Chapter 27: The Pupil of the Marshalsea

In the Marshalsea, Clennam realises that the example by which he guided his efforts to order his life to good was that of Little Dorrit. However, it requires the self-sacrifice of John Chivery, who triumphs over his own sentimental absurdity, to reveal to Clennam the astonishing fact of his having been the object of her love, so that he becomes conscious of having suppressed something in his dealing with her as if she were a child. Visited by the Plornishes, he persuades himself that his separation from Little Dorrit has been for the best in keeping her free of his fall; but he realises that she has been the object, 'the centre of the interest of his life', the end of all his good.

NOTES AND GLOSSARY:

equal to your weight: Chivery is contemplating a boxing-match
simoom: a hot North African wind
green meat: meat: originally any solid food
Upas tree: Javanese tree, said to poison the whole area around it
Goliath: a giant (killed by David: see the Bible, I Samuel 17)
Mooshattonisha padrona: it much astonishes the lady
Tuscan: Tuscany is celebrated for the purity of its Italian

Chapter 28: An Appearance in the Marshalsea

After some three months, Clennam is visited by Ferdinand Barnacle, who sympathetically hopes that the Office was not responsible for his downfall, but defends its and Merdle's humbug. He is succeeded by Rigaud-Blandois-Lagnier, disguised as a soldier, who has been tracked down by Cavalletto. He has been in hiding to put pressure on Mrs Clennam, to whom he wishes to sell something, and while Pancks carries a message to her, Rigaud defends his own mercenary attitude as essentially that of society: he has been employed by Miss Wade to spy on the Gowans. Pancks now returns with Flintwinch, who is authorised to agree to Rigaud's demands, and to make an appointment for the following week. Clennam's own powerlessness leaves him feeling even more miserable.

NOTES AND GLOSSARY:

Giant . . .windmill: in Miguel de Cervantes's (1547-1616) novel *Don Quixote* (1605), Part 1, Chapter 8, Don Quixote charges a windmill, thinking it a giant
Phoebus: Apollo, the sun god
Salve!: (*Latin*) Hail!

Chapter 29: A Plea in the Marshalsea

As the week passes, Clennam's physical health worsens as his despondency at imprisonment deepens. On the sixth day, he awakens from a fitful dream to find fresh flowers on his table, placed there by Little Dorrit, who, wearing her old clothes, has returned to her father's old room to offer Clennam tender comfort. Her presence brings peace and fortitude, though he refuses to purchase his liberty by accepting her money to pay his debt: he believes he has irrevocably lost the right to do this by his failure to understand his secret self in the days of her poverty; and his fortitude enables him to ask her to look forward in her own life rather than back to his. After her departure, however, John Chivery brings her message of 'undying love'.

Chapter 30: Closing in

On the appointed day Rigaud, accompanied by Pancks and Cavalletto, goes to meet Mrs Clennam. Arthur's friends are sent away, but Mrs Flintwinch rebels against the 'clever ones' and insists on hearing and speaking during the crucial interview, to which Mrs Clennam fatalistically agrees. Rigaud has offered to sell her compromising papers, originally for one and now for two thousand pounds. To bring her to his price, he offers fragments of the Clennam family history over several generations, supplemented by Affery's recollections of what she has heard in her 'dreams'. This produces an outburst from Mrs Clennam, who passionately defends her actions according to her distorted religion, becoming in the process partially liberated from her chronic paralysis. Finally, Flintwinch in his turn breaks his restraint, contradicts her account of her motives, and adds his own share of information. (As the extremely complex prehistory of the novel is revealed in a fragmentary way, it is presented separately below, reordered to assist comprehension.) Rigaud presses his demand by revealing that if Mrs Clennam does not buy the papers by midnight, Arthur and Little Dorrit will read copies of them. In the crisis, Mrs Clennam rises from her chair and runs into the street, leaving Rigaud calmly triumphant in the house. (The one mystery unsolved is that of the mysterious rustlings Affery hears in the house.)

NOTES AND GLOSSARY:

Knight of Industry: (*French*: Chevalier d'industrie) adventurer, crook

spirted it: shot it

Mr Beelzebub: Lord of the Flies, prince of evil spirits (reinforcing the suggestions of Rigaud's devilishness)

Nemesis: the Greek goddess of retribution
Jehovah: the unutterable name of God in Hebrew scripture
gammon: (*colloquial*) nonsense
Lucifer: name for Satan, as rebel against God
Jezebel: a bold woman (see the Bible, I Kings 18)
not to be burnt on a Sunday night: strict observance of the Sabbath precluded business, and even the lighting of fires

Summary of the facts revealed in Book 2, Chapter 30
Arthur Clennam's father was a timid orphan brought up in isolation from the world by his stern uncle Gilbert, who chose for him a wife similarly educated in a gloomy religion of 'wholesome repression'. Within a year, Mrs Clennam discovered that her husband had gone through a form of marriage with a young singer, by whom he had a child, Arthur. Conceiving herself the instrument of divine punishment, Mrs Clennam agreed to support the singer in a life of self-reproach, on condition that she held no communication with the father and gave the child to be brought up as Mrs Clennam's son (who in his turn was educated in 'fear and trembling' for sin).

Gilbert Clennam, at the point of death, relented towards his nephew's beloved, and dictated to Mrs Clennam a codicil to his will, leaving a thousand guineas to the girl, and a thousand to the youngest daughter of her patron or his brother. Since it was Frederick Dorrit who had encouraged the singer, the legatee would therefore be Little Dorrit. Mrs Clennam, as her husband knew, suppressed (but did not destroy) the codicil to prevent 'sin' being rewarded, though she later did befriend Little Dorrit. It was this suppression to which Arthur's father, separated for many years in China, drew attention in sending her the watch with the paper monogrammed D.N.F.: she was not to forget to make restitution (as Arthur guessed) rather than, as she chose to interpret it, to continue to punish sin. (Dickens's number-plan for the serialisation of the novel makes it clear that the paper was originally marked by Arthur's mother, and therefore originally a reminder to his father of their mutual love.) In the interval, Mrs Clennam became paralysed, and on Arthur's return had to rely on Flintwinch to burn the concealed codicil, which he in fact kept.

Arthur's real mother, long dead, had gone mad and had been kept in the care of Flintwinch's twin-brother Ephraim, who had passed to Jeremiah her papers. It was these, together with the codicil, which Jeremiah returned in an iron box to Ephraim (as seen by Affery in Book 1, Chapter 4), after Arthur came back from China. Ephraim went to Antwerp, where he became acquainted with Rigaud, who got hold of the contents of the iron box, now the instruments of his blackmail of Mrs Clennam, after Ephraim's death.

Chapter 31: Closed

In the twilight, the wild figure of Mrs Clennam makes her way in the unfamiliar outside world to the Marshalsea, where she finds Little Dorrit and asks her to read the paper left by Rigaud. She promises restitution to the confused girl whom she asks to be merciful in not disclosing the story to Arthur at least until after her death, so that she will not lose the respect so sternly inculcated in his childhood. Little Dorrit, in response to this talk of anger and vengeance, appeals to the values of compassion and forgiveness, and agrees to go with Mrs Clennam to appeal to Rigaud not to give Arthur the hurtful information. They hurry through the unusually peaceful evening, only to find the Clennam house, just as they reach it, suddenly collapse, crushing Rigaud. (Flintwinch is absent, having fled to the Continent with the firm's money.) Mrs Clennam collapses, and never again moves or speaks in her remaining three years of life.

NOTES AND GLOSSARY:

innocent perished with the guilty: see Genesis 18:23 on the destruction of Sodom

the healer of the sick, the raiser of the dead: Little Dorrit's references to Jesus reinforce her image as the embodiment of the spirit of the New Testament ('later and better days'), which is picked up in 'crown of thorns'; the following images of light and shade emphasise the contrast between the two women

Chapter 32: Going

While Clennam lies ill in prison, Pancks becomes increasingly restless as he broods on his calculations that led to the fatal investment. Pressed by Casby to squeeze even more money out of Bleeding Heart Yard, he goes there before his proprietor, finally rebels, and denounces him as a 'philanthropic sneak' before the assembled Yard. This he follows with the even more effective act of cutting off Casby's flowing locks, which reduces him to a grotesque butt of laughter.

NOTES AND GLOSSARY:

peruke: wig, or hair-covered skull-cap

after Dr Johnson: 'we that live to please, must please to live' (*Prologue spoken at Drury Lane,* 1747)

Stop: device to bring into play the pipes of an organ (hence 'one tune . . . Grind')

Chapter 33: Going!

While Fanny, Sparkler, Mrs General and Mrs Merdle continue in their foolish old ways, Little Dorrit loyally devotes herself to the imprisoned Clennam; at her request, Mr Meagles searches Rigaud's haunts on the Continent for the originals of the crucial papers. He has no sooner reached the Marshalsea to report on a useless interview in Calais with Miss Wade, than Tattycoram enters, bearing the box of papers, with which she has run away, begging for forgiveness and readmission to the Meagles household, and rejecting Miss Wade's power over her. Mr Meagles recommends to her as a model of behaviour the unselfish, dutiful Little Dorrit. (The latter meanwhile is willing that Clennam should eventually know all his own story, but not the story of her own legacy, lost through Mrs Clennam.) Mr Meagles decides to go abroad to bring back Daniel Doyce to help free Clennam from the prison.

NOTES AND GLOSSARY:

came out of her furnace: like the Jews who would not worship the gold statue (see the Bible, Daniel 3)

Nelson: Horatio, Lord Nelson (1758-1805), one of greatest British naval heroes, triumphant against Napoleon

nailing [colours] to the mast: in obstinate defiance

Standard of four Quarterings: emphasising his family connections by the coats of arms on his heraldic shield

Diligence days: see Book 1, Chapter 11 (a reminder of the period the novel is set in)

Chapter 34: Gone

On an animated autumn day Clennam, still in prison, hears in Little Dorrit's reading the voice of Nature, but, anticipating his release, tells her they must part. When he again refuses to share her fortune she reveals that all the money Fanny and Mr Dorrit had was invested in Merdle's schemes, and that she is now as poor as before: her riches and fulfilment are in her future life with Clennam. At this moment, Flora Finching arrives and comically but sincerely, with best wishes to Little Dorrit, resigns her hopes for Clennam. Some time later, Mr Meagles returns, bringing Doyce, who has been honoured abroad for his public achievements. Doyce puts Arthur's financial error down to experience, offers him his old position in the firm, and announces his release from the Marshalsea. The following morning, having at Little Dorrit's request burned a paper unread (Rigaud's blow against him), Clennam leaves the prison for the church where, in the presence of their friends, they are at last married. The last glimpse is of them going quietly out 'inseparable and blessed' into the restless world of the 'roaring streets'.

NOTES AND GLOSSARY:

like a clog-hornpipe: quickly and noisily: a hornpipe is a lively dance; wooden-soled clogs were used in certain dances

Sibyllic: like the prophetess or witch of mythology

crossed: a word-play: Doyce is not thwarted as in England, but rewarded with medals of honour (as in 'starred')

Britannia in the Manger: the common expression is 'dog in the manger', meaning one who will not let others enjoy something he himself has no use for; here, restrictive of other countries' attitudes as well as her own

women's nightcaps: Mr Meagles persists in his failure (typical of his class and time) to take foreigners very seriously

Saint Paul's Churchyard: where a special marriage licence could be had at Doctors' Commons

third volume of our Registers: perhaps a glance at what had become the standard three-volume format for nineteenth-century novels, many of which did carry the hero from birth in the first to marriage in the third (part-serialisation, as of this novel, was the major exception)

Part 3

Commentary

WHEN DICKENS BEGAN WORK in early 1855, it was on a novel to be called *Nobody's Fault* in which, as his biographer Forster reports, the leading man was to 'bring about all the mischief in it, lay it all on Providence, and say at every fresh calamity, "Well, it's a mercy, however, nobody was to blame, you know" '. In the course of his work on the early chapters, it struck him that

> it would be a new thing to show people coming together, in a chance way, as fellow-travellers, and being in the same place, ignorant of one another, as happens in life; and to connect them afterwards, and to make the waiting for that connection a part of the interest.

Although neither of these ideas was fully followed through, elements survive in the titles of chapters 16, 17, 26, 28 ('Nobody's Disappearance') and in, for example, the meetings at the Great St Bernard (Book 2, Chapter 1). Eventually Dickens identified his main narrative strands and principal characters, in recognition of which the work in progress was by the fourth number retitled *Little Dorrit*.

The topical element

The original conception of 'Nobody' was related to the social criticism in the novel. *Little Dorrit* is a very topical work; although imprisonment for debt and the speculating mania are appropriate to the 1820s, the main thrust of the reference is to the period of the novel's appearance. The opening of Chapter 3 was written to a background of rioting in June 1855 against a Bill for rigid Sunday observance; the railway boom of the mid-1840s, the rise of joint-stock companies and financial giants, had both led to some widely publicised disasters for small investors: the suicide in February 1856 of the fraudulent John Sadleir, MP (alluded to in the Preface), merely crystallised Dickens's existing 'general idea'. The political dimension of the novel contains many references to the circumstances of the early 1850s, a time of unstable governments compounded of 'Barnacles' and 'Stiltstalkings', whose premier representative, Lord Decimus, is a caricature of Lord Palmerston, Prime Minister since January 1855, and a frequent target of Dickens's attacks for his obstructive indifference to the pressing need for government action.

The Circumlocution Office, in which the Barnacles figure so prominently, is a compound of Civil Service and Parliamentary Government through ministers. In 1853 the Northcote-Trevelyan report had identified many ills in the Civil Service, including the pushing into office, through the personal or political connections of their families, of the incompetent, the self-interested, the well-born idler. The war which Britain fought against Russia in the Crimea in 1854-6 revealed with appalling clarity the inefficiency and corruption which had led to military disaster and great human suffering: everyone has heard of the futile Charge of the Light Brigade, and of the distress of the ordinary soldiers until adequate nursing care was provided by Florence Nightingale. As Dickens remarks in the Preface, a Commons committee was already at work (since January 1855) investigating the administration of the war; Dickens himself spoke on behalf of the new Administrative Reform Association and supported his friend A. H. Layard, MP, whose parliamentary motion for reform, obstructed by Palmerston, was rejected after a debate echoed in Chapter 10 of Book 1 of the novel, which Dickens described as 'blowing off a little of indignant steam'. In his journalism he attacked a system in which 'Nobody' was ever found responsible for the maladministration or took the initiative in clearing it up; so widespread was the malaise that he believed that 'the English people are habitually consenting parties to the miserable imbecility into which we have fallen, and never will help themselves out of it'. Little wonder that in October 1855, having just written Chapter 10, he could comment: 'I have no present political faith or hope—not a grain'. By this stage in the writing, he had realised that his criticisms would be best expressed not by pinning all the responsibility on one man as originally planned, but by ranging widely within his society to illustrate a decayed system. His social diagnosis therefore had important artistic consequences, discussed below, for the construction of the novel.

The serialisation of *Little Dorrit*

One reason why Dickens was able to include particularly topical elements in the novel was his continued preference for the serial method of writing and publishing which had been successful ever since *Pickwick Papers* in 1837. In Dickens's day, novels were most commonly published in three volumes at ten shillings and sixpence each, a considerable sum for the average person; his substitution of monthly shilling numbers reduced the overall price, spread it over a longer period of time, and made his fiction available to a wider public (the average monthly sale of *Little Dorrit* was some thirty three thousand, to which must be added later sales in volume form). The novel was published between December 1855 and June 1857 in eighteen monthly numbers at one shilling and a final double number at two shillings, the standard procedure: the purchaser got a pamphlet with a green illustrated cover, containing thirty-two pages of text (usually three or four chapters), two illustrations, and advertisements for general goods (which suggest that the publishers had in mind a largely middle-class market). The original monthly parts each contained several chapters beginning in Book 1 with Chapters 1, 5, 9, 12, 15, 19, 23, 26, 30, 33, and in Book 2 with Chapters 1, 5, 8, 12, 15, 19, 23, 27, 30.

Although it is clear from the notes Dickens made in the plans for the individual numbers of his novels that, especially in his later career, he had worked out an overall scheme, he had usually only written three or four numbers when the first one was published, and by the end of a novel he would be working just ahead of the printers. If this seems a very risky method, it was successful in stimulating his imagination, it allowed the inclusion of topical material, and it allowed him to develop details of plot or character in response to his readers' reactions as expressed in sales, letters and reviews: as the Preface shows, Dickens was very aware of a special relationship with his public, and was anxious to carry it with him from one project to the next. Instead, then, of reading one fat volume in several days or weeks as we do, the original audience of *Little Dorrit* lived with it for eighteenth months, waiting to see how it would evolve; this is at least part of the explanation for some of the artistic techniques Dickens uses.

Dickens talks in his Preface of 'weaving' and 'threads', which we may understand more clearly if we compare a serialised novel to the modern television serial. In both, the writer has to bear in mind that it is some time since his audience last encountered the plot and characters. To help it to 'find its feet' he may therefore provide a strong gripping plot (if it involves mystery or suspense, so much the better, as people will want to come back to see how it is resolved); vividly drawn characters, often readily identifiable by their speech or appearance; and a variety of mood, tone, and incident, because a serial works in shorter units and at a different pace from a single long novel, play, or film. In a novel such as *Little Dorrit*, which contains many major characters, he must be careful not to let any single group drop out of view for so long that the reader cannot remember how it fits into the whole. The creation of a serious novel in this form therefore involves preserving a delicate balance between the overall structure and the needs of the individual numbers, which may often end on a note of suspense. You might consider for yourself how a particular month's number forms a unit: in the fifteenth number, for instance, (Book 2, Chapters 15-18) we have an opening scene in Rome, where the Dorrit and Merdle families are linked by marriage; the arrival in London, where Mr Dorrit is taken up by Mr Merdle to new heights; a reminder through Flora Finching of the dark mystery involving Mrs Clennam and Rigaud; a reminder through John Chivery of the past which Mr Dorrit is trying to throw off; and his dream-filled return to Italy, with foreshadowings of his collapse in the next number. Within this variety, Dickens creates ever tighter links between the Merdle, Dorrit and Clennam families, which have consequences for plot and theme.

The illustrations, although often selectively or poorly reproduced in cheap editions, were not a casual afterthought: many years of collaboration with H. K. Browne ('Phiz') had taught Dickens their value, since they were not only an attractive incentive to purchasers, but could illustrate, clarify, even extend the details of the written text. Dickens's correspondence shows him regularly taking a close interest in the grouping, gestures, dress of characters, and instructing 'Phiz' in the use of recurrent symbolic images. The original title-page of this novel, for instance, shows Little Dorrit herself at the dark gate of the prison, with a shaft of sunlight on her; the letters of the title are made of heavy stone blocks, and metal bars linked by metal chain. The coloured wrappers of the monthly parts surrounded similar details with an elaborate allegorisation of the main themes of the novel: the bottom has a bustling crowd of travellers jostling each other; at the left, a sleeping man sits in an armchair on top of a crumbling tower, against which leans a falling tree, while above the entrance a pair of rats frame a coat of arms; at the right, a decayed, overgrown church topped by a raven is the background to Mrs Clennam in her wheelchair, accompanied by Flintwinch, while to their side a boy leapfrogs a tombstone; at the top, a procession goes in the opposite direction to a signpost; it is led by blind cripples, fools, and a fashionable gentleman; a despondent or sleeping Britannia is pushed in her bathchair by men in fools' hats followed by creeping and fawning hangers-on; at the back is a shadowy group of women and children. The whole picture touches on the political and religious themes of the novel through a series of details which anticipate many images of the text.

Structure and plot

Most novels tell a story, but there is much more to them than that. Out of the raw materials he is considering, the author must choose those which he thinks will fit together, he must decide where to begin and end, what relative importance to give to specific episodes and characters, and how the story is to be told; all of these will affect our sense of what the novel is about. In the second half of his career, in *David Copperfield* (1850) and *Great Expectations* (1861), Dickens created first-person narrators using the benefit of adult hindsight to look back at their own childhood: 'I saw . . . , I said . . . '. Shortly before our novel, in *Bleak House* (1853), he had made the experiment of alternating throughout the novel between a first-person narrator writing in the past tense of experiences in which she was involved and a third-person narrator writing about many of the same characters in a more detached way in the present tense: 'Jo stops and looks . . . '. Dickens was well aware of the different kinds of impact to be gained by different narrative methods, so we must examine closely the distinctive features of *Little Dorrit* before we come to talk of themes.

At first sight, there is no obvious centre in the novel to which everything else is related: even Clennam, the most likely candidate, only intermittently seems aware of parts of the action. In the opening numbers, we find what look like separate stories involving groups of characters not closely related: Rigaud and Cavalletto in prison; Clennam, the Meagles family, and Miss Wade, briefly meeting in quarantine; Mrs Clennam and the Flintwinches in the old house; the Dorrits in the Marshalsea; the Barnacles in the Circumlocution Office; the inhabitants of Bleeding Heart Yard; the Casby household; to these are later added Merdles and others. We are initially uncertain how to respond to all these, as the narrative offers more questions than answers: part of the difficulty for the reader is that the mystery and suspense elements are carefully maintained by Dickens until at the last moment he provides an elaborate series of explanations, going back forty years, in Book 2, Chapter 30. If, however, we regard the stories of the separate groups as the 'threads' of the 'pattern' to which he refers in the Preface, we may see that he gives hints early on as to the weaving process. Miss Wade speaks more truth than she realises, in Chapter 2:

> '. . . you may be sure that there are men and women already on their road, who have their business to do with *you*, and who will do it. Of a certainty they will do it. They may be coming hundreds, thousands, of miles over the sea there; they may be close at hand now; they may be coming, for anything you know or anything you can do to prevent it, from the vilest sweepings of this very town.'

This foreshadows the relationships of Miss Wade with the Meagleses, of Clennam with Pet, and of Rigaud (lying nearby in prison) with all of them.

The early numbers identify Clennam as the principal 'thread', by following which we are introduced to several of the main locations of the novel and offered further links between them: his visit to his mother's house almost casually brings in the quiet figure of Little Dorrit, interest in whom leads him to the Marshalsea and her family;

his concern for her father takes him to the Circumlocution Office, where Mr Meagles is reintroduced, and Doyce established, which in turn leads Clennam to Bleeding Heart Yard, the property of Casby, father of his former sweetheart, Flora Finching. As the plot develops, we find that Casby, the former agent of Lord Decimus Tite Barnacle, has 'confidential agency business' with Miss Wade, who pays Rigaud to spy on the Gowans. Rigaud in his turn is linked to Cavalletto, who ends up in Bleeding Heart Yard, and to the Clennam family by his getting the crucial papers following the fortunate death of Flintwinch's twin-brother. Having initially been puzzled by a series of questions about events and motivations—why is Miss Wade disdainfully aloof? What is the explanation of Affery's dream? What wrong is there in the Clennam past and how could Little Dorrit be connected with it? What is Mr Merdle's complaint? What will Pancks's enquiries turn up about the Dorrits?—the reader is almost overwhelmed with answers which provide a close 'weaving' of the lives of the characters, especially when the dénouement reveals that the connection between the Dorrit and Clennam families, established through old Frederick and Arthur's real mother, goes back forty years. By the end of the novel, then, we realise that the seemingly disparate elements have been integrated into a complex plot. To the modern reader it may seem that some of the links mentioned above, and others such as Rigaud's second meeting with Cavalletto (in Book 1, Chapter 11) or the meeting of Mrs Merdle and the Dorrits at the Continental hotel (Book 2, Chapter 3) are very implausible. It is true that the plot of the novel depends very much on the apparatus of mysteries and coincidences which Dickens inherited from the eighteenth-century novel and from popular theatre (see 'The literary background' in Part 1 above); but the proper concern for the critical reader is to ask what positive use Dickens makes of his inheritance. Through these devices, for instance, he produces a plot which allows him to range from the exotic scenes of Rome and Venice, the fashionable world of Mrs Merdle, the aristocratic world of the Barnacles, the professional and financial world of the Merdle hangers-on, to the Marshalsea, the French prison, Bleeding Heart Yard, and the casual miseries of London by night; this plot is not simply held together by overlapping groups of characters, but is continuously reinforced by devices of repetition and imagery, discussed below.

Within the social and geographical diversity noted above, there is a simple basic structure: the titles of the two Books—'Poverty' and 'Riches'—reflect the gain in material fortune of the Dorrit family. But these also have an ironic value, as by the end of the novel the two old men are dead, Tip has been seriously ill, Fanny is uneasily married, and all the fortune has been lost through Merdle's schemes; the only real happiness lies with Amy, who has never been comfortable with the family values, and is finally united in her poverty with Clennam, who has himself fallen from comparative riches in Book 1 to imprisonment for debt in Book 2: their final 'riches' are clearly spiritual in nature. Clennam's end provides further evidence of structuring in the novel, as he has spent several months, attended finally by Little Dorrit, in the very room where she so long watched over her father (Book 2, Chapter 29). This similarity of situation invites us to compare the two men—how they come to be there, how prison affects them, how they face up to their responsibilities, how they recognise the value of Little Dorrit herself. Even allowing for the vast difference in the time they spend there, we can see that Mr Dorrit settles down to a life of self-deception and pretence about his dependence on his daughter, while Clennam, who has chosen to go there by honourably taking on himself the blame for the firm's failure, comes to recognise the significance to him of Little Dorrit:

> Looking back upon his own poor story, she was its vanishing-point. Everything in its perspective led to her innocent figure. He had travelled thousands of miles towards it; previous unquiet hopes and doubts had worked themselves out before it; it was the centre of the interest of his life; it was the termination of everything that was good and pleasant in it (Book 2, Chapter 27)

This is one example of a device used frequently by Dickens to strengthen the organisation of the novel: while the line of the plot carries us forwards, he uses parallels or contrasts between pairs or groups of characters to remind us of what has gone before and to bind individuals into a more generalised view of the world. The rather ineffectual Clennam, for instance, is put into partnership with the eminently practical Doyce, who in his turn is contrasted with the complacently condescending 'practical' Meagles, and with the Barnacle determination 'not to do it'; the quiet selflessness of Little Dorrit is contrasted with her shallow sister, with the tortured anger of Miss Wade and Tattycoram, and with the cold worldliness of Mrs Gowan and Mrs Merdle; when Rigaud in Book 2, Chapter 28 suggests that Clennam could never be a gentleman such as he is, Dickens is pointing up a theme which has been extensively explored through the aspirations of Mr Dorrit, the idling of Gowan and the Barnacles, and the ambiguous position of Mr Merdle, whose suicide provokes from his Chief Butler the pronouncement that 'no ungentlemanly act on Mr Merdle's part would surprise' him. You will be able to think of other examples of such devices of repetition and variation which use the individual examples as parts of the larger pattern. (Think, for example, about the characters' attitudes to marriage and to money.) This use of correspondence also works with the links established through coincidence and the development of the plot to give a sweeping unified view of the society under scrutiny.

Even within the basic structure of the novel there are devices which reinforce its unity, as individual episodes anticipate, parallel, or comment on others. When the jailer's daughter, like an angel in the prison, visits the cell in Chapter 1, she has an instinctive 'dread' of Rigaud echoed in other characters, in the aggression of Gowan's dog, and most deeply felt (in Book 2, Chapter 7) in the intuitive response of Little Dorrit and Pet: 'an aversion amounting to the repugnance and horror of a natural antipathy towards an odious creature of the reptile kind'. Clennam's miserable night in the Marshalsea in Chapter 8 anticipates his longer, enforced stay in Book 2; his carrying Little Dorrit insensible from the prison at the end of Book 1 is mirrored at the end of Book 2 by an exit which is only possible for him because of her spiritual strength. Flora Finching's 'mysterious signalling, expressing dread of discovery' in Book 1, Chapter 13 of the 'secret understanding' between herself and the bewildered Clennam is like a parody of the more serious mystery he is half aware of in his past. When Mr Dorrit in Book 1, Chapter 31 sees it as his 'public duty' to respond to the request that he 'preside over the assembled Collegians' in the Marshalsea, he echoes Mr Merdle's acceptance of the 'duty that he owed to Society' to 'come among us' as proposed by Treasury, in Chapter 21. Dickens thus deflates the pretensions of Merdle's toadies and prepares for the exposure of Merdle as a criminal. Once again, you will be able to find other examples for yourself.

If the organisation of *Little Dorrit* is not at first sight as straightforward as the story of a single character's life, whether told in the first or the third person, this does not necessarily make it any less coherent or unified. The remarks above suggest that Dickens very skilfully works towards an end in which the various elements are indeed seen as parts of a single whole: it is one of his contributions to the novel as a form that he is able to develop out of the sometimes hackneyed traditions on which he draws an organisation which does not limit his material to one character or group: in *Little Dorrit* he offers an analysis of a complex modern society in a state of change, illustrating not just its diversity but, through the parallels and coincidences, the interrelatedness of its parts, so that characters are not seen as totally independent or acting in isolation; their actions are modified by forces beyond their own control, of which they may even be unaware, and they in their turn may have unforeseeable impact on the lives of others. If this is obvious in the treatment of the Circumlocution Office or Merdle's financial operations, it seems also to be true of the most intimate aspects of life: Miss Wade's comments already quoted might apply ominously to the disruptive force of Rigaud in several lives, but they might also be taken more hopefully to initiate what the narrator, as early as Chapter 9 of Book 1, calls the 'destined interweaving' of the stories of Clennam and Little Dorrit, a destiny finally recognised by Clennam at the end of Book 2, Chapter 27, when he sees her as the end of his journey. But even this moment, private as it is, is presented by Dickens in imagery which once again makes connections throughout the novel, and redirects us towards a general theme. It is to this function of the imagery that we now turn.

Imagery

Like the plot features and the parallels of situation mentioned above, the imagery of the novel is used by Dickens to point up the connections between groups of characters and areas of interest, and to direct us towards ways of interpreting the basic story. One of the things which a plot summary almost entirely omits is a sense of the precise detail in which characters and situations are presented; but in most novelists, and certainly in a highly metaphoric writer like Dickens, the exact means of imaginative expression—such as the use of simile, metaphor, or symbol—is of the greatest importance, not only because the comparisons expressed or implied make the detail more vivid, but because in combination they can help us see beneath the initial level of 'story' to that of 'theme', which is normally more difficult to define. A novel can be 'about' several things simultaneously: *Little Dorrit* is obviously about the lives of the characters invented by Dickens, but they are also used as examples of whole areas of society of his time, and we might in the end feel that the essential themes of the novel have an application to the human condition well beyond the framework of the situations Dickens begins with. Imagery, then, can once again be a unifying device.

We have seen above how some of the illustrations refer to specific images or situations in the novel. The title page, for instance, shows Little Dorrit in a shaft of sunlight against the dark background of the prison gate. As soon as we turn to the text, we find even in the title of Chapter 1, 'Sun and Shadow', a variant on this image, which is developed in the contrast between the intense light of the 'great flaming jewel of fire' in the sky, and the dark rot of the prison, so foul that even the sun seems to refuse to enter; some seventy chapters later Clennam and Little Dorrit leave the church after their marriage, look out in 'the autumn morning sun's bright rays', and in the novel's last sentence, pass along 'in sunshine and shade'. These are examples from many dozens of variants of this imagery, which is applied to many characters and situations; from the first chapter, Rigaud—the true criminal—is associated with darkness, while Cavalletto becomes 'sunny';

other sources of negation are included: Clennan haunts the 'shady waiting-rooms of the Circumlocution Office' (2, 10), and sees the whole neighbourhood of his mother's house 'under some tinge of its dark shadow' (2, 10), which may be related to the 'shadow of a supposed act of injustice, which had hung over him since his father's death' (27)*; Mr Merdle's ominous complaint is a faint shadow compared to that of the Marshalsea wall, which 'was a real darkening influence, and could be seen on the Dorrit Family at any stage of the sun's course' (21); Mr Meagles leaves Miss Wade in Calais, 'taking his honest face out of the dull room, where it shone like a sun' (2, 33). These examples show that sometimes there is an initial literal reference in the 'sun' and 'shadow'; sometimes it is primarily metaphoric: another use appears in Little Dorrit's story of the tiny woman who guarded the shadow of someone who had gone away (24). By extension, shadowing and the removal of light become associated with many of the unhealthy forces in the novel: Little Dorrit can see that the fiction about the Gowan family's attitude to Pet's marriage 'had its part in throwing upon Mrs Gowan the touch of a shadow under which she lived' (2, 7); and, in one of the central examples of the image, she recognises in her father's insensitive attitude the continuing contamination of his life: 'in his whole bearing towards her, there was the well-known shadow of the Marshalsea wall. It took a new shape, but was the old sad shadow' (2, 5). Such imagery runs through the novel, often coming to greater prominence at moments where Dickens wishes to display contrasts in values, like the confrontation in Book 2, Chapter 31, just before the collapse of the house kills Rigaud; in this, the contrasting appeals of Mrs Clennam and Little Dorrit to the spirits of the Old and New Testaments conclude: 'In the softened light of the window, looking from the scene of her early trials to the shining sky, she was not in stronger opposition to the black figure in the shade than the life and doctrine on which she rested were to that figure's history.' In the last page of the novel, this symbolic value of the image is again clearly pointed up: 'They were married with the sun shining on them through the painted figure of Our Saviour on the window.'

It is clear from these examples that one image or chain of images cannot be considered totally in isolation: here the light and shade are ways of heightening aspects of contrasting values worked out through plot and character, which they vary as well as repeat. Not all recurring images run throughout the novel: you might think for yourself which images relate to the Marseilles jailer's reference to his 'birds' (1); to the 'caged birds' of the Marshalsea (36), of which Clennam becomes one (2, 27); and to Mrs Merdle's remarkable parrot with its golden

*Throughout this section numbers in brackets refer to chapters in Book 1 unless indicated otherwise.

cage (20). Is Mrs Merdle's celebrated snowy bosom (21) related to the 'noble Refrigerator' of the Circumlocution Office (26)? Are Pet Meagles's roses, launched on the river by Clennam (28), echoed in the 'blooming nosegay' from Little Dorrit which revives him in prison (2, 29)? (And what about the name 'Flora' for his earliest attachment?)

Clennam's disposal of Pet's roses links them to another group of images, centred on the river, which are used by Dickens particularly to show Clennam's feelings about his own life: increasingly aware that he is middle-aged, and that his love for Pet would not be returned, he thinks 'it might be better to flow away monotonously, like the river, and to compound for its insensibility to happiness with its insensibility to pain' (16); the 'flowing road of time' (16) becomes an image by which to suggest his lack of emotional progress (his self-pity is parodied in John Chivery's pastoral fancy to 'glide down the stream of time' with Little Dorrit (18)); Clennam's fears about the family secrets are represented by his image of himself as a criminal on a boat watching the river flow over the body of his immovable victim, like the 'shifting current of transparent thoughts and fancies' (2, 23). (Compare Little Dorrit in Venice (2, 3), thinking of the 'lasting realities' of her life as she muses on the Grand Canal.)

The 'flowing road' naturally reminds us of the images of travel in the novel, such as we have already seen in Miss Wade's speech (2), and in Clennam's realisation that he has been travelling towards Little Dorrit (2, 27); she is in fact the answer to his doubts as to where he is driving 'on the darker road of life' (26). These images should come as no surprise, since the illustrated wrapper had featured a crowd of harassed travellers against a background of distant ships, and the action includes the return of Clennam from China as well as the comings and goings of many of the main characters between London and the Continent. The natural figurative extension of the literal reference takes us to old Mr Dorrit in prison, 'like a passenger aboard ship in a long voyage' (19), and even to Flora's moral lesson that 'all the paths in life are similar to the paths down in the North of England where they get the coals and make the iron and things gravelled with ashes' (2, 23). Although some of these images allow for the possibility that the journey has no particular destination, others suggest an element of organisation or shaping: Miss Wade's ominous comment might suggest predetermined journeys, Clennam's realisation in Book 2, Chapter 27 is that unconsciously he has in fact had a goal, beyond making reparation for any family wrong, in his 'journey of life': Little Dorrit as his 'centre of interest' has been the object of a quest in which the 'destined interweavings' the narrator refers to have gradually taken place in their lives. Clennam's journey has a reward in a wife who is a compound of practical helper, emotional support, and religious symbol; it is a successful version of the religious journey of trial or expiation on which the narrator sees all mankind engaged:

> And thus ever, by day and night, under the sun and under the stars, climbing the dusty hills and toiling along the weary plains, journeying by land and journeying by sea, coming and going so strangely, to meet and to act and react on one another, move all we restless travellers through the pilgrimage of life. (Chapter 2)

You might consider how Clennam's gradual awakening to the fact that his journey has a destiny could be connected to Dickens's working out of the elaborate plot in a way which eventually fuses the initially random-seeming elements into a controlled structure with significance for the themes of the novel. In Chapter 15, writing of Mrs Clennam's room, he echoes his earlier images to give us a hint:

> Strange, if the little sick-room fire were in effect a beacon fire, summoning some one, and that the most unlikely some one in the world, to the spot that *must* be come to. Strange, if the little sick-room light were in effect a watch-light, burning in that place every night until an appointed event should be watched out! Which of the vast multitude of travellers, under the sun and the stars . . . may, with no suspicion of the journey's end, be travelling surely hither? Time shall show us.

The most obvious group of images in *Little Dorrit* is, of course, the one Dickens develops out of the idea of imprisonment. We first encounter the 'prison taint' in Marseilles, with 'the imprisoned air, the imprisoned light, the imprisoned damps, the imprisoned men . . . all deteriorated by confinement'. But the quarantine of Chapter 2 seems little better, as Mr Meagles complains of the 'shutting up' and sees his group as 'jail-birds'. Clennam's first London Sunday is in a 'bolted and barred' city, whose present inhabitants want only a 'stringent policeman', whose former inhabitants might in ghostly form 'pity themselves for their old places of imprisonment'. With memories of his boyhood Sundays, when he was marched to chapel 'morally handcuffed' or saw the bound Bible with an ornament 'like the drag of a chain', he visits his mother who sits, almost guarded by Flintwinch, in her gloomy room, restricted by a paralysis which seems to be a reflection of her spiritual state, the result of self-imposed moral bondage (3). Temporarily shut in the Marshalsea (8), Clennam later wonders whether his mother's confinement may be a penalty for her responsibility for Mr Dorrit's captivity. Early in the novel, then, we are prepared to see uses of this imagery radiate out from the original literal sense.

The dominant prison imagery in the novel comes from the Marshalsea itself, whose influence on the Dorrit family is so strong that it permeates even the Continental scenes of Book 2: the iron grates of the Great St Bernard remind Little Dorrit of a prison, though they do not give her the anxiety that the ideas of contraction and confinement do to her father (2, 1); she finds 'the descent into Italy, the opening of that beautiful land as the rugged mountain-chasm widened and let them out from a gloomy and dark imprisonment—all a dream—only the old mean Marshalsea a reality' (2, 3); even in Venice, with its 'dungeon-like' tenements, where they live in a palace 'six times as big as the whole Marshalsea' but no more homely, and where the Gowans live above rooms 'with barred windows, which had the appearance of a jail for criminal rats', the experience of tourism is in a long passage interpreted by Little Dorrit as being parallel to the family's earlier experiences: 'they were brought into these foreign towns in the custody of couriers and local followers, just as the debtors had been brought into the prison.' In short, 'this same society in which they lived, greatly resembled a superior sort of Marshalsea' (2, 7). So intense is the Marshalsea infection that Mr Dorrit in particular never really escapes from the 'living-grave', finally conducting himself in his last days as though really still in it: 'The broad stairs of his Roman palace were contracted . . . to the narrow stairs of his London prison' (2, 19).

As we have seen, these images are not applied only to those who are literally imprisoned: as a man of discretion, Mr Chivery 'locked himself up as carefully as he locked up the Marshalsea debtors'; the unfeeling Mrs Merdle has a chin 'curbed up so tight and close by that laced bridle'; her husband's secret is anticipated in his pose, 'with his hands crossed under his uneasy coat-cuffs, clasping his wrists as if he were taking himself into custody' (33) (his Chief Butler seems a Society-appointed warder, much as Mrs General is the custodian of the Dorrit proprieties). Other prisons include Old Nandy's Workhouse (31), and the 'dreary red-brick dungeon at Hampton Court' where Mrs Gowan lives; the Circumlocution Office is like a police-station or a place of torture for convicts (2, 8; 10). This extension of the imagery beyond the literal prison once again serves to unify the various areas of society within a single view: within a frequently gloomy and repressive world the individual may be cramped by particular laws or social customs, by corrupt institutions, by warped values. Many of the examples above show, however, that the individual is not simply the victim of outside forces: Mr Dorrit's self-deception about his position in the Marshalsea has brought him to a point where he hardly recognises the truth of his own condition; Miss Wade's own account of her life shows that its deceit is indeed 'self-torment'; Mrs Gowan and Mr Merdle are in their different ways figures of conscious deception;

Mrs Clennam in her 'cell of years' admits, 'while I am shut up from all pleasant change I am also shut up from the knowledge of some things that I may prefer to avoid knowing' (15), her paralysis as much a refuge as an expiation; even Arthur himself is in part a prisoner of a situation created before his birth.

This analysis suggests that the metaphor of the prison becomes a representation of a state of mind which conceals or refuses to admit reality; from the criminal deception of Merdle, through the eye-averting fictions so necessary to Mrs General and polite 'Society', to the pathetic condition of the Dorrits, there is an essential continuity of attitude, which is opposed by those characters identified by the majority as threats. There is Doyce, with his power 'of explaining what he himself perceived, and meant, with the direct force and distinctness with which it struck his own mind' (2, 8); and, above all, Little Dorrit with what her family see as an unfortunate concern with reality: ' "we can always go back to the plain truth." "Yes, but if you please we won't," retorted Fanny' (2, 6). The liberation of Clennam comes only after his recognition of the reality embodied in Little Dorrit; by the end of the novel, truth has at least been revealed in the climax of Book 2, Chapter 30 with its dramatic revelations, and in the symbolic nakedness of the dead Merdle, the shearing of the humbug Casby; even the 'controllable pictures' of Mrs Clennam's imagination are challenged by the 'overwhelming rush of the reality' (2, 31). The more closely we look, the more tightly bound together do we find plot, image and theme. As we saw above, *Little Dorrit* has a highly topical element, but one function of the recurrent imagery is to modify that by its power to connect and generalise: if at one level the novel is 'about' topics like the recent laws on debt, it is in the end more importantly about the general human condition, which Dickens sees as threatened by 'the prison of this lower world' (2, 30).

Characterisation

One of the reasons for Dickens's continuing popularity is his power to create vivid characters who are memorable in themselves and also embody many of the novels' themes. A novel of wide range such as *Little Dorrit* contains dozens of characters, not all of whom can be discussed here in detail: but it is necessary to look at the methods Dickens uses in some examples, since they vary in their importance in the novel as a whole and in the way he creates them.

Many of the simplest characters in the novel help to create the background, the social context of the main stories, and are not seen as fully rounded individuals. The group surrounding Mr Merdle—Bar, Horse Guards, Treasury, Bishop—are known only by the names of their professions and characteristic attitudes and speech; Bar, for instance, 'with his little insinuating Jury droop, and fingering his persuasive double eye-glass', carries his professional manner into private conversation: 'he would venture to suggest that the question arose in his mind . . . '. Here we see simple examples of two principal means of characterisation used by Dickens: the use of a kind of speech which distinguishes an individual or group; and the use of description, whether of physical appearance and gesture or of surroundings. The Barnacles, by whose name the reader is forewarned, though they all have their idiosyncrasies, are linked by their gentlemanly use of many words to say little: 'It is competent to any member of the—Public . . . to memorialise the Circumlocution Department. Such formalities as are required to be observed in so doing, may be known on application to the proper branch of that Department.'

Many of the most prominent characters are conceived in a similar way, although by the end of the novel some of them are revealed in a new light or changed attitude. We remember Mrs Clennam sitting rigidly in her dark room misusing the language of religion: 'The world has narrowed to these dimensions, Arthur . . . . It is well for me that I never set my heart upon its hollow vanities.' Daniel Doyce is 'merely a short, square, practical looking man, whose hair had turned grey, and in whose face and forehead there were deep lines of cogitation, which looked as though they were carved in hard wood . . . . He had a spectacle-case in his hand, which he turned over and over while he was thus in question, with a certain free use of the thumb that is never seen but in a hand accustomed to tools.' His brief, unaffected speech helps mark him out as the natural enemy of the word-bound Barnacles: a serviceable idea is 'put into his head to be made useful'. (Compare Doyce and Mr Meagles in Chapter 16 at the cottage, whose cultural lumber makes it 'like the dwelling of an amiable Corsair': Clennam, despite his affection, is allowed to see the limitations of Meagles as he condescends as a 'practical' man to the 'crotchety' engineer.)

Other figures are characterised through speech or appearance: Mrs Merdle's cynical acceptance of Society's arbitrary values ('we know it is hollow and conventional and worldly and very shocking') is outwardly presented in the cold snow of her 'broad unfeeling handsome bosom'; her husband, in contrast, 'had not very much to say for himself; he was a reserved man, with a broad, overhanging watchful head . . . and was mostly to be found against walls and behind doors'. You should select several characters and list for yourself how Dickens follows up initial descriptions of this sort: Pancks, for instance, is first seen by Clennam puffing and blowing 'like a little labouring steam engine', an image which then becomes the 'little coaly steam-tug' to the unwieldy Casby. Rigaud is several times identified by the reader simply by his speech, with its stress on gentlemanliness and its literal rendering of French idioms, and by his appearance: 'His moustache went up under his nose, and his nose came down over his moustache, in a very sinister and cruel manner.' Mr Dorrit's halting speech hints not only at the enfeebling effects of the prison, but at the contamination of the relationship between language and reality: 'I make that remark, because it is not to be doubted that my son, being by birth and by — ha — by education a — hum — a gentleman, would have readily adapted himself to any obligingly expressed wish on the subject of the fire being equally accessible to the whole of the present circle. Which, in principle, I — ha — for all are — hum — equal on these occasions — I consider right.' The example of Mr Dorrit shows, of course, that Dickens is not confined by this method of characterisation to the portrayal of unchanging characters. Mr Dorrit retains various idiosyncrasies until his death, but the tragedy of his life is gradually explored as he fails to distance himself from the Marshalsea; he is in addition seen through the eyes of several other characters, within and without his own family.

In his characterisation, therefore, Dickens often isolates a few leading features of an individual, and keeps returning to them, often in a heightened form, which some readers may feel makes them seem very unrealistic. Against this, we might say that it makes characters memorable over the long original serialisation; that it is actually true to much of our own experience, in which we see only certain recurring aspects of each other's lives; that Dickens, as the discussion of plot and imagery shows, is not a realistic novelist anyway; and that some of the characters are really quite complex. If, for instance, Dickens makes fun of John Chivery's pastoral fantasies, he balances this with his honest help to Clennam in the Marshalsea; Flora Finching is a comic creation to rank with the Dickens immortals ('ere we had yet fully detected the housemaid in selling the feathers out of the spare bed Gout flying upwards soared with Mr F. to another sphere'), but her ludicrous sentimentality is also a comment on Clennam, and is balanced by her good-hearted promotion of the qualities of Little Dorrit. (Dickens seems more concerned here than in many of his earlier novels to prevent our responding in a very simple way to characters of this sort.)

The principal figures in the novel are, of course, Clennam and Little Dorrit, who are portrayed by rather different means from the others. Clennam is discussed in Section 4; here we will consider the problem of whether Little Dorrit is simply too improbable to be an effective character. As we have seen, she appears to Clennam as the ideal towards which he has been striving; but this truth is only gradually realised. She is not vigorously caricatured; rather, the real strength of her unobtrusive character is quietly revealed through the course of the action, as it is contrasted with her unpromising origins:

> With no earthly friend to help her, or so much as to see her, but the one so strangely assorted; with no knowledge even of the common daily tone and habits of the common members of the free community who are not shut up in prisons; born and bred in a social condition, false even with a reference to the falsest condition outside the walls; drinking from infancy of a well whose waters had their own peculiar stain, their own unwholesome and unnatural taste; the Child of the Marshalsea began her womanly life.

Her character is partly defined by contrast with what she is not: her self-deceiving father, selfish sister, the hypocritical society represented by Mrs General, and, above all, Rigaud, whose satanic associations are presented in images which contrast with her religious values. Her smallness and physical vulnerability help to point up her spiritual integrity and her symbolic function: episodes like the meeting with the prostitute (Chapter 14) and the unexpected gentleness of Mrs Clennam (Chapter 29) emphasise her special qualities. If the narrator sometimes seems to sentimentalise her child-like qualities, this is set against the more penetrating presentation of her character in Book 2, where we view Italy partly through her eyes, and read her own accounts in her letters to Clennam. There remains a curious duality about her role as child-protector of her father, of Maggie, and of Clennam, with whom she has an unerotic relationship which seems to owe as much to social convention as to individual character; but it is as the completion of his journey, as the refutation of the lying and hypocrisy of society, that she has her value in the novel: Dickens deliberately creates her character through means which help mark her differences from those other, more 'fixed' characters, whose very rigidity mirrors the entrapment of the potentially free spirit in 'the prison of this lower world'. In the corrupt world, she becomes an unlikely source of strength to Clennam, as the wheel turns full circle: she 'nursed him as lovingly, and GOD knows as innocently, as she had nursed her father in that room when she had been but a baby'.

(There is not space here to do justice to the vitality and range of Dickens's language in both narration and dialogue: you can compile further examples of your own of its various aspects discussed above.)

Part 4

Hints for study

THE HISTORICAL BACKGROUND and the summaries above are no substitute for careful reading (preferably more than once) and consideration of the novel itself. As you read, you should jot down reminders of the kind of detail that will come in useful in critical discussion, where you may have to say not just *what* happens, but *how* it is presented by the author. (The chapter summaries above omit, for instance, the methods by which character and theme are revealed.) Try to summarise your own impressions of the book *before* reading any secondary works: this is valuable critical training. One way of deciding what is distinctive about Dickens would be to compare the plot, characterisation, and language of other novelists you have read, such as Jane Austen, the Brontës, Hardy.

The best general preparation for an examination is to become really familiar with the text and think about the main aspects of the author's technique. These vary according to the literary form being considered, but in a novel they will usually include: plot, narrative method, setting, characterisation, theme, as well as choice of language and imagery. To support your views on these topics, you will need either to quote the words of the text or be able to refer in some detail to points within it. Thinking about the author's method, once you have become familiar with the story and characters, may come in two stages: analysis, in which you identify in isolation the features listed above; and synthesis, in which you see how they work together in the novel as a whole to define exactly what it is about. Do not try to learn passages from critical writing or load your work with jargon: simple, direct writing about what you really know is far more convincing than pretentious elaboration.

Consideration of the various headings listed will be easier if you have been systematic in taking note of useful examples. Even under 'narrative method' where it is clear that the story is told in the past tense by someone standing outside the action, you should have noted down, for instance, the occasions where Little Dorrit and Miss Wade are allowed to express themselves directly in written documents; the way in which the final revelations come not through the voice of the narrator but from the characters gathered in Mrs Clennam's house; the fact that Dickens allows us no direct access to the minds of most characters—especially the caricatured or 'stereotyped'—but does allow us to know what Clennam and Little Dorrit are thinking and feeling (this is also relevant to the discussion of characterisation).

Several of these topics are discussed in Section 3 above; you should consider how you might develop or modify the accounts there, as well as familiarise yourself with the few technical terms commonly used which might crop up in an examination. A question about the 'plot' of *Little Dorrit* might require you to examine how Dickens has constructed a complex whole out of several different stories involving the Dorrits, Clennams, Merdles, Meagleses and so on, some of which might tend to pathos, some to comedy, some to social satire. How is the structure organised to emphasise certain episodes rather than others, and what methods are then used for the effects within them? Try the test of asking yourself which episodes you find most memorable, and what in the writing makes them so: it might be Clennam at the Circumlocution Office; Little Dorrit and Maggy in the London streets; the travellers at the Great St Bernard; or Little Dorrit in Venice. What matters is that you should work from *what* to *how*, and develop an awareness of artistic techniques. Some examination questions may simply ask you to summarise an episode or describe a character; but you are more likely to be asked about authorial method: perhaps to comment on one of the features discussed in Part 3, or to 'evaluate' or 'comment critically' on them; you may be offered a critic's opinion about the work, with which you need not wholly agree or disagree. You should always justify your opinion by reference to the text: while you cannot carry all the details in your head, you should at least remember the broad sequence of events and relationships, turning-points such as dramatic confrontations between characters (for example, Book 2, Chapter 30), striking portraits (Flora Finching, Flintwinch), the main varieties of language used to create mood and character, some examples of the unifying metaphors. (In the rare cases where the text is allowed in the examination room, much more exact and specific reference to it is normally expected. Certain kinds of essay, such as close analysis of a set passage, are only possible if the text is available.)

There is such a thing as good examination technique. Find out what your examination regulations require; it is useful to consult old papers to see the kinds of phrasing used: some examples are given below. If you have to write several answers within a limited time, you must learn to draw on your knowledge of the text to construct a planned argument, clearly answering a specific question, making effective use of detail. The best way to do this is to practise writing specimen answers under similar conditions, so that you submit complete and relevant essays. In an examination you should (a) read the instructions and questions carefully, making sure you know what is asked for;

(b) choose a topic for which you have raw material, and plan the outline of the whole essay, giving an ordered structure which will lead you to a final view of the topic; (c) write the essay to your plan, using quotation or detailed reference to the text to support the critical ideas you offer: there is unlikely to be a simple right or wrong answer; a well-ordered and accurate analysis is what will impress. If you have prepared several different kinds of material (such as plot, character and so on), you should be able to draw on and adapt some of them for almost any question. (It is usually best to write about the novel in the present tense.) Listed below are some specimen questions requiring different kinds of approach (you may find some useful pointers in Part 3).

Specimen questions

1. Describe a selected character within the novel. [A more complex topic is his 'role' or 'function' which requires consideration of his place in the structure and themes of the novel as a whole: see the discussion of Pancks below.]
2. How successful is Dickens in linking the stories of the Dorrit and Clennam families?
3. Discuss (with examples) the use of description and setting in the novel.
4. Analyse the use of two parallel or contrasting characters and their relation to the themes of the novel. [There are many possible combinations here: see Part 3 on structure.]
5. What in your view constitutes Dickens's standard for judging morality in the novel?
6. Illustrate the novel's variety of mood from comedy to tragedy.
7. How does Dickens treat the governing classes or the family in the novel? Discuss several examples of either.
8. Write a critical estimate of Dickens's handling of Clennam or Little Dorrit. Would you agree that they are unconvincing?
9. What is the function of the mystery element, and how does it affect the organisation of the plot?
10. 'The perversion of language is one of this novel's main themes.' Discuss with reference to the variety of the language Dickens employs.

Below you will find specimen answers to a few additional specimen questions (in an examination you would probably have space to elaborate individual points).

Specimen answers

1. The character and role of Pancks.

Pancks is the rent-collector for the hypocrite Casby, in whose house Clennam first meets him. Short, dark, very dirty and always puffing, he seems like an engine, or a steam-tug towing his proprietor. In this capacity he is efficient, perhaps to the point of ruthlessness as he spreads terror among the tenants of Bleeding Heart Yard and gains a harsher reputation than his master. But his mysterious behaviour in Book 1 gradually reveals another side to his character: as the 'gipsy fortune-teller', he spends his own time and money working to prove Mr Dorrit heir to an unclaimed fortune, which leads to a turning-point in the action—Mr Dorrit's release from the Marshalsea.

Despite his gentler private side, Pancks is a completely practical man, as the mechanical imagery suggests: he never reads anything but letters and accounts, and sees it as his natural function to 'keep always at it'. The limitation of this practical attitude is seen in his 'infection' by an absolute belief in Merdle's schemes, in which he invests his own money and fatally persuades Clennam to plunge Doyce's, thus being the unwitting instrument of Clennam's committal to the Marshalsea: failing to learn from the deceits of Casby, he is obsessed by his calculations which 'prove' the solidity of Merdle. He advises Clennam: 'Be as rich as you honestly can. It's your duty. Not for your sake, but for the sake of others.'

After the crash, violently reproaching himself for his persuasions, he acts for the imprisoned Clennam and, when his arithmetic cannot explain Merdle's deceit, finally exposes Casby as a humbug before his tenants in the Yard, thus rejecting the abuse of his practical talents which he eventually turns to better use as chief clerk and then partner in the firm of Doyce and Clennam. Despite seeming grotesque, Pancks is at heart a decent man who has been partly warped by the sordid commercial world by whose values he lives and eventually suffers. He is used by Dickens to further several aspects of the plot, and reinforce the analysis in the novel of the dangerous effect of false values. Although presented largely from the outside, he is not a simple black-and-white figure; in his 'practicality' and final honesty, he is to be set against many other characters in the novel.

2. Analysis of a selected passage: the description of Mrs Clennam's dining-room and bed-chamber in Chapter 3.

This description is presented through the consciousness of Clennam who not only observes the present but is reminded of the past. The dark dining-room has no association of joyful boyish meals: the 'hard-featured clock' speaks of the stern lessons which warped his youth. The furniture suggests sterility and death: the empty closet, used for punishment, seems the entrance to Hell; the empty cellaret, a coffin; even the pictures illustrate the plagues of vengeance familiar in his mother's Old Testament wrath. The death imagery continues as Clennam goes to her room: the mourning tablet panels, the bier-like sofa, the 'block at a state execution', prepare us for her widow's dress. The lack of spontaneous love in his repressive childhood is recalled in his mother's 'glassy kiss' and 'stiff fingers' (again death-like), while the rigidity of her life is emphasised in the unchanging nature of the room; even the vitality of the fire lies under 'damped ashes'. (Much of the imagery connects with the larger symbolic patterns which run through the novel.)

The description can be seen as characterising both Mrs Clennam, who lives among these objects, and Clennam himself, who is both a product of this environment and the perceiving mind whose melancholy state it reflects (the chapter has been steeped in gloom up to this point). The darkness, decay, apartness from the world, combine to portray Mrs Clennam entombed in the rigidity of her 'religious' self-deception; they remind us of other prisons in the novel, even of the dilapidated and desolate palaces of Italy. In the Clennam house, with its grotesque retainers (including the 'hanged' Flintwinch), the objects seem to have more life than the people: the fire has drawn out the dye from the dress; the clock is personified as a 'savage' and 'growling' master.

The detail, vivid in itself, is part of Dickens's characterisation; the linking of details shows how carefully the imagery through the novel is worked out, and contributes to our understanding of the themes. The detail clarifies the Clennam family relationships and points to the decay of the firm as an economic unit (compare the impressive surroundings of Merdle): the 'sunk and settled' floor reinforces this theme, but also prepares us for the moment, hundreds of pages later, when Dickens completes the weaving of the 'pattern' and produces, out of the decay and the mysterious noises, the final collapse of the house, of the firm, of Rigaud, and of Mrs Clennam's false values.

---

3. Discuss Arthur Clennam as the hero of *Little Dorrit*.

Many of the novels by which Dickens was influenced centred on the adventures of young, vigorous, sometimes rather immoral heroes. There is, however, much in *Little Dorrit* which is not directly a part of the story of Clennam, while he seems an unlikely hero, aged forty, and the victim of others. In Chapter 2, he tells Mr Meagles how his repressive and materialist parents blighted his inner life even before his 'exile' in China: 'Will, purpose, hope? All those lights were extinguished before I could sound the words.' Clennam's story is not one of bold action, but of his inner growth and painful acquisition of self-knowledge as his spark is rekindled in the presence of Little Dorrit.

Dickens often represents Clennam as a 'dreamer' and perhaps criticises the self-pity of his middle-aged romantic fancy for Pet Meagles, while providing the warning figure of his decayed early love, Flora Finching: Clennam's casting himself as 'Nobody' seems to be a flight from admitting reality. But Chapter 13 shows how the dream is rooted in 'a belief in all the gentle and good things his life had been without'; its closing words show how he is unknowingly close to the source of spiritual renovation in Little Dorrit, although happiness only comes when at the end of the novel he can recognise the nature of his feelings for her. In the middle of the novel, having cast her in the role of 'adopted daughter', he gives her pain by seeing her merely as a standard of 'fortitude and self-command'; these qualities at least confirm him in the more active life he has begun in rejecting his mother's firm, taking up the causes of Mr Dorrit and Doyce with the Circumlocution Office, and entering the factory, though the shadow of the family past hangs over him: 'he must begin, in practical humility, with looking well to his feet on Earth, . . . he could never mount on wings of words to Heaven. Duty on earth, restitution on earth, action on earth; these first, as the first steep steps upwards.'

By giving us access to Clennam's thoughts, Dickens presents him in greater complexity and psychological depth than most other characters. The imagery of travel makes his life a quest for the destined goal, not in material prosperity, but in personal fulfilment with Little Dorrit. Clennam is also the focus of many of the social and moral themes and of the imagery; he is marked out by his integrity, purified by his suffering. His happiness is a private end; he does not change the world which, as the closing paragraph shows, continues heedless of the values he has learned from Little Dorrit. (You might consider the question of the parent-child relationship, sometimes inverted, between Clennam and Little Dorrit, especially as it parallels that with her father.)

Part 5

Suggestions for further reading

The text

Quotations from the novel are based on the 1868 text, with reference by book and chapter number, to allow use with any edition. There are many cheap modern editions, including the Penguin, Penguin Books, Harmondsworth, 1967, with notes and a London map; and the World's Classics edition, Oxford University Press, Oxford, 1982, with notes and Dickens's number plans. The standard scholarly edition, with an introduction on the writing of the novel, is Volume IV of the Clarendon Dickens, Clarendon Press, Oxford, 1979.

Other works by Dickens

You might enjoy reading other novels of the second half of Dickens's career, such as *Bleak House* (1853); or the first-person narratives, *David Copperfield* (1850) and *Great Expectations* (1861); or the very different methods of the early novels, *Pickwick Papers* (1837) and *Nicholas Nickleby* (1839).

Background information can be found in his extensive non-fiction: in his journalism; correspondence (*The Letters of Charles Dickens,* ed. W. Dexter, 3 vols, Nonesuch Press, London, 1938; to be superseded by the Pilgrim edition); speeches (*The Speeches of Charles Dickens,* ed. K. J. Fielding, Oxford University Press, Oxford, 1960).

Biography

FORSTER, JOHN: *The Life of Charles Dickens,* 3 vols, 1872-4. Various editions. A long account by a friend and literary adviser, reproduces primary documents.

JOHNSON, EDGAR: *Charles Dickens: His Tragedy and Triumph,* Gollancz, London, 1953. Long, scholarly, draws on more sources than Forster.

WILSON, ANGUS: *The World of Charles Dickens,* Secker and Warburg, London, 1970 (Penguin paperback, 1972). Biography and criticism, with many contemporary illustrations.

Background and critical works

BUTT, JOHN and TILLOTSON, KATHLEEN: *Dickens at Work,* Methuen, London, 1957. On serialisation; Chapters I and IX especially.

FIELDING, K. J.: *Charles Dickens, A Critical Introduction,* Longman, London, 2nd ed., 1965. Brief account of career.

HOUSE, HUMPHRY: *The Dickens World,* Oxford University Press, London, 2nd ed., 1942. Pioneer work on social background.

LEAVIS, F. R. and LEAVIS, Q. D.: *Dickens the Novelist,* Chatto and Windus, London, 1970. Chapter 5 on *Little Dorrit* and Blake.

MILLER, J. HILLIS: *Charles Dickens: The World of his Novels,* Oxford University Press, London, 1958. Influential American view.

MONOD, SYLVERE: *Dickens the Novelist,* University of Oklahoma Press, Oklahoma, 1968. An elaborate critical work.

WALL, STEPHEN (ED.): *Charles Dickens* (Penguin Critical Anthologies), Penguin Books, Harmondsworth, 1970. Shows development of Dickens criticism from contemporary to modern.

The author of these notes

IAN MCGOWAN is a native of Glasgow. He read English at the University of Oxford and is a Lecturer in English Studies at the University of Stirling.

YORK NOTES

The first 200 titles

		Series number
CHINUA ACHEBE	*A Man of the People*	(116)
	Arrow of God	(92)
	Things Fall Apart	(96)
ELECHI AMADI	*The Concubine*	(139)
JOHN ARDEN	*Serjeant Musgrave's Dance*	(159)
AYI KWEI ARMAH	*The Beautyful Ones Are Not Yet Born*	(154)
JANE AUSTEN	*Emma*	(142)
	Northanger Abbey	(1)
	Persuasion	(69)
	Pride and Prejudice	(62)
	Sense and Sensibility	(91)
SAMUEL BECKETT	*Waiting for Godot*	(115)
SAUL BELLOW	*Henderson, The Rain King*	(146)
ARNOLD BENNETT	*Anna of the Five Towns*	(144)
WILLIAM BLAKE	*Songs of Innocence, Songs of Experience*	(173)
ROBERT BOLT	*A Man For All Seasons*	(51)
CHARLOTTE BRONTË	*Jane Eyre*	(21)
EMILY BRONTË	*Wuthering Heights*	(43)
JOHN BUCHAN	*The Thirty-Nine Steps*	(89)
ALBERT CAMUS	*L'Etranger (The Outsider)*	(46)
GEOFFREY CHAUCER	*Prologue to the Canterbury Tales*	(30)
	The Franklin's Tale	(78)
	The Knight's Tale	(97)
	The Merchant's Tale	(193)
	The Miller's Tale	(192)
	The Nun's Priest's Tale	(16)
	The Pardoner's Tale	(50)
	The Wife of Bath's Tale	(109)
	Troilus and Criseyde	(198)
SAMUEL TAYLOR COLERIDGE	*Selected Poems*	(165)
WILKIE COLLINS	*The Woman in White*	(182)
SIR ARTHUR CONAN DOYLE	*The Hound of the Baskervilles*	(53)
JOSEPH CONRAD	*Heart of Darkness*	(152)
	Lord Jim	(150)
	Nostromo	(68)
	The Secret Agent	(138)
	Youth and *Typhoon*	(100)
DANIEL DEFOE	*Moll Flanders*	(153)
	Robinson Crusoe	(28)
CHARLES DICKENS	*A Tale of Two Cities*	(70)
	Bleak House	(183)
	David Copperfield	(9)
	Great Expectations	(66)
	Nicholas Nickleby	(161)
	Oliver Twist	(101)
	The Pickwick Papers	(110)

		Series number
JOHN DONNE	*Selected Poems*	(199)
THEODORE DREISER	*Sister Carrie*	(179)
GEORGE ELIOT	*Adam Bede*	(14)
	Silas Marner	(98)
	The Mill on the Floss	(29)
T. S. ELIOT	*Four Quartets*	(167)
	Murder in the Cathedral	(149)
	Selected Poems	(155)
	The Waste Land	(45)
WILLIAM FAULKNER	*Absalom, Absalom!*	(124)
	As I Lay Dying	(44)
	Go Down, Moses	(163)
	The Sound of the Fury	(136)
HENRY FIELDING	*Joseph Andrews*	(105)
	Tom Jones	(113)
F. SCOTT FITZGERALD	*The Great Gatsby*	(8)
E. M. FORSTER	*A Passage to India*	(151)
ATHOL FUGARD	*Selected Plays*	(63)
MRS GASKELL	*North and South*	(60)
WILLIAM GOLDING	*Lord of the Flies*	(77)
OLIVER GOLDSMITH	*She Stoops to Conquer*	(71)
	The Vicar of Wakefield	(79)
GRAHAM GREENE	*The Power and the Glory*	(188)
THOMAS HARDY	*Far From the Madding Crowd*	(174)
	Jude the Obscure	(6)
	Selected Poems	(169)
	Tess of the D'Urbervilles	(80)
	The Mayor of Casterbridge	(39)
	The Return of the Native	(20)
	The Trumpet Major	(74)
	The Woodlanders	(160)
	Under the Greenwood Tree	(129)
L. P. HARTLEY	*The Go-Between*	(36)
	The Shrimp and the Anemone	(123)
NATHANIEL HAWTHORNE	*The Scarlet Letter*	(134)
ERNEST HEMINGWAY	*A Farewell to Arms*	(145)
	For Whom the Bell Tolls	(95)
	The Old Man and the Sea	(11)
HERMANN HESSE	*Steppenwolf*	(135)
BARRY HINES	*Kes*	(189)
ANTHONY HOPE	*The Prisoner of Zenda*	(88)
WILLIAM DEAN HOWELLS	*The Rise of Silas Lapham*	(175)
RICHARD HUGHES	*A High Wind in Jamaica*	(17)
THOMAS HUGHES	*Tom Brown's Schooldays*	(2)
ALDOUS HUXLEY	*Brave New World*	(156)
HENRIK IBSEN	*A Doll's House*	(85)
	Ghosts	(131)
HENRY JAMES	*Daisy Miller*	(147)
	The Europeans	(120)
	The Portrait of a Lady	(117)
	The Turn of the Screw	(27)
SAMUEL JOHNSON	*Rasselas*	(137)

		Series number
BEN JONSON	*The Alchemist*	(102)
	Volpone	(15)
RUDYARD KIPLING	*Kim*	(114)
D. H. LAWRENCE	*Sons and Lovers*	(24)
	The Rainbow	(59)
	Women in Love	(143)
CAMARA LAYE	*L'Enfant Noir*	(191)
HARPER LEE	*To Kill a Mocking-Bird*	(125)
LAURIE LEE	*Cider with Rosie*	(186)
THOMAS MANN	*Tonio Kröger*	(168)
CHRISTOPHER MARLOWE	*Doctor Faustus*	(127)
	Edward II	(166)
SOMERSET MAUGHAM	*Of Human Bondage*	(185)
	Selected Short Stories	(38)
HERMAN MELVILLE	*Billy Budd*	(10)
	Moby Dick	(126)
ARTHUR MILLER	*Death of a Salesman*	(32)
	The Crucible	(3)
JOHN MILTON	*Paradise Lost I & II*	(94)
	Paradise Lost IV & IX	(87)
	Selected Poems	(177)
V. S. NAIPAUL	*A House for Mr Biswas*	(180)
SEAN O'CASEY	*Juno and the Paycock*	(112)
	The Shadow of a Gunman	(200)
GABRIEL OKARA	*The Voice*	(157)
EUGENE O'NEILL	*Mourning Becomes Electra*	(130)
GEORGE ORWELL	*Animal Farm*	(37)
	Nineteen Eighty-four	(67)
JOHN OSBORNE	*Look Back in Anger*	(128)
HAROLD PINTER	*The Birthday Party*	(25)
	The Caretaker	(106)
ALEXANDER POPE	*Selected Poems*	(194)
THOMAS PYNCHON	*The Crying of Lot 49*	(148)
SIR WALTER SCOTT	*Ivanhoe*	(58)
	Quentin Durward	(54)
	The Heart of Midlothian	(141)
	Waverley	(122)
PETER SHAFFER	*The Royal Hunt of the Sun*	(170)
WILLIAM SHAKESPEARE	*A Midsummer Night's Dream*	(26)
	Antony and Cleopatra	(82)
	As You Like It	(108)
	Coriolanus	(35)
	Cymbeline	(93)
	Hamlet	(84)
	Henry IV Part I	(83)
	Henry IV Part II	(140)
	Henry V	(40)
	Julius Caesar	(13)
	King Lear	(18)
	Love's Labour's Lost	(72)
	Macbeth	(4)
	Measure for Measure	(33)
	Much Ado About Nothing	(73)

		Series number
WILLIAM SHAKESPEARE *(continued)*	*Othello*	(34)
	Richard II	(41)
	Richard III	(119)
	Romeo and Juliet	(64)
	Sonnets	(181)
	The Merchant of Venice	(107)
	The Taming of the Shrew	(118)
	The Tempest	(22)
	The Winter's Tale	(65)
	Troilus and Cressida	(47)
	Twelfth Night	(42)
GEORGE BERNARD SHAW	*Androcles and the Lion*	(56)
	Arms and the Man	(12)
	Caesar and Cleopatra	(57)
	Major Barbara	(195)
	Pygmalion	(5)
RICHARD BRINSLEY SHERIDAN	*The School for Scandal*	(55)
	The Rivals	(104)
WOLE SOYINKA	*The Lion and the Jewel*	(158)
	The Road	(133)
	Three Short Plays	(172)
JOHN STEINBECK	*Of Mice and Men*	(23)
	The Grapes of Wrath	(7)
	The Pearl	(99)
ROBERT LOUIS STEVENSON	*Kidnapped*	(90)
	Treasure Island	(48)
	Dr Jekyll and Mr Hyde	(132)
JONATHAN SWIFT	*Gulliver's Travels*	(61)
JOHN MILLINGTON SYNGE	*The Playboy of the Western World*	(111)
W. M. THACKERAY	*Vanity Fair*	(19)
DYLAN THOMAS	*Under Milk Wood*	(197)
J. R. R. TOLKIEN	*The Hobbit*	(121)
MARK TWAIN	*Huckleberry Finn*	(49)
	Tom Sawyer	(76)
VOLTAIRE	*Candide*	(81)
EVELYN WAUGH	*Decline and Fall*	(178)
JOHN WEBSTER	*The Duchess of Malfi*	(171)
	The White Devil	(176)
H. G. WELLS	*The History of Mr Polly*	(86)
	The Invisible Man	(52)
	The War of the Worlds	(103)
ARNOLD WESKER	*Chips with Everything*	(184)
	Roots	(164)
PATRICK WHITE	*Voss*	(190)
OSCAR WILDE	*The Importance of Being Earnest*	(75)
TENNESSEE WILLIAMS	*The Glass Menagerie*	(187)
VIRGINIA WOOLF	*To the Lighthouse*	(162)
WILLIAM WORDSWORTH	*Selected Poems*	(196)